TRAAST+GRUSON

Exposed

Birkhäuser – Publishers for Architecture
Basel · Boston · Berlin

Frame magazine
Amsterdam

Everything in the world exists in order to end up in a book.

Stéphane Mallarmé

I.
INTRODUCTION

We enter the world of Ewoud Traast and Edith Gruson. A world of irony and wit, good sense and gumption.

School time in the Netherlands. Landscapes and
cityscapes clotted with wheeling clusters of kids
shouldering book bags and backpacks on their way
to and from school. Dense packs of young cyclists. It's
a familiar scene. And for the Dutch, a memorable detail
of their school-going days.

'I always met my friends at the bridge,'
says Edith, *'and we biked to school together. Back and forth.*
Every day.'

Edith is Edith Gruson.
Her partner is Ewoud Traast.
TRAAST + GRUSON.

They established their partnership in
1986 and, since that time, have completed more than
thirty design projects together: museum exhibitions,
commercial and thematic expositions, cultural and civic
events.

ISBN 90-806445-4-4

9 789080 644540 >

They met at school, at the Art Academy in Rotterdam.

They had a thing once, then. Edith and Ewoud.
They also created and organized things together. Student parties. Social events.
It came naturally to them.

Edith entered the Art Academy in Rotterdam with the intention of
studying interior architecture, but graduated with a degree in
graphic design and photography.

'*Door handles and window treatments don't excite me,*' she
admits. '*I'm interested in atmosphere, in creating a space to be in.*'
She emphasizes the verb to be. '*And, at the same time, in giving
that space a reason to be.*'

I obviously look puzzled.

'*Subjective space,*' she says. '*I want the space I design to
accommodate and accentuate the actions and interactions of those
who use it—to give them all the more reason to be there.*'

'*Experiential space,*' I offer.

'*Yes,*' she agrees. '*You could call it that.*'

'*We have piles of firewood in the garden,*' she continues.
'*It's a space we love and use a lot. We build fires there, even during
the summer months. A simple fire changes the whole experience of
being in the space. And it changes the nature of the space as well.*'

I nod, imagining a nocturnal scene painted with glowing
firelight, curling flames licking the air, the crackling sound of
burning logs, the heady scent of wood smoke... and the warmth
of the fire.

1999. A design competition sponsored by HEMA, a Dutch department store that sells quality consumer products at affordable prices.

—————Backpacks.

—————The subject conjures up images of

—————peddling packs of school-bound kids.

—————A visual cliché in Holland.

The pictogram of an elongated bicycle, painted on streets and appointed pavements to indicate bikeways, is translated into a life-size cutout. Mounted on the handlebars of each bike is a prototype backpack designed for the competition, now on display.

The winning design is, appropriately, leader of the pack.

The bike pictogram originated in Holland. And, as I've said, school in Holland is associated with packs of bikes. The design elements—the exposition's visual lexicon, so to speak—are unmistakably Dutch. While the exposition could be staged at a foreign venue, the emotive impact of the clichéd images would be lost on those for whom biking, Dutch-style, is not part of their personal experience.

Subjective experience. This is what Edith had been talking about.

Using visual clichés as a starting point, as they did here, TRAAST + GRUSON capitalize on the shared personal experiences of their audience.

They start from a place of memory.

Recall, if you will, Magritte's Treason of Images:

Ceci n'est pas une pipe.

7

If it's not a pipe, what is it?
'A painting,' *the painting answers.*
A sign that denotes an object and triggers memory.
The work of TRAAST + GRUSON *proclaims:*
This is not reality.
Ewoud entered the Art Academy in Breda to study photography. After a time he became dissatisfied and transferred to the Art Academy in Rotterdam to follow a broader curriculum. (He met Edith there.)

'While the practice of photography is broad enough,' he explains, 'I found that my interest lay in its application, in using it in combination with other media. I could manipulate form, light, and shadow to create the illusion of space and could apply the image to a two-dimensional form. A poster, for example.'

Ewoud found he was able to exercise his penchant for staging—an aspect of the photographer's art that he loves—in his collaborative projects with Edith.

'The work we do, which centers on visual communications, is not tied to any one medium,' he says. 'So our vocabulary is extremely broad.'

As a discipline, visual communications might be thought of as design that bridges the gap between aesthetic and everyday experience.
It is a telling.

—————It is a vehicle.

—————It is a subject as well as an object.

—————A noun and a verb.

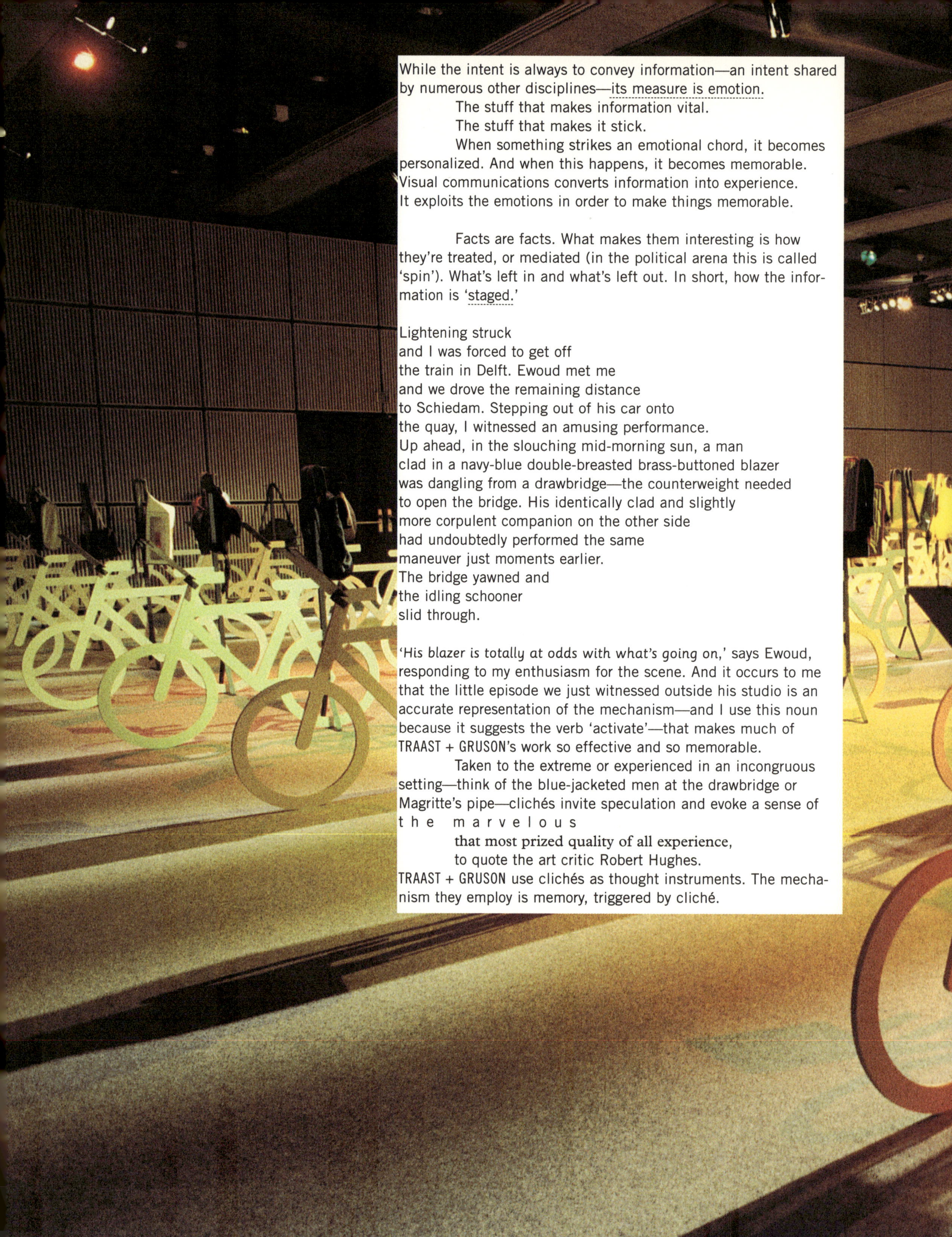

While the intent is always to convey information—an intent shared by numerous other disciplines—its measure is emotion.
     The stuff that makes information vital.
     The stuff that makes it stick.
     When something strikes an emotional chord, it becomes personalized. And when this happens, it becomes memorable. Visual communications converts information into experience. It exploits the emotions in order to make things memorable.

     Facts are facts. What makes them interesting is how they're treated, or mediated (in the political arena this is called 'spin'). What's left in and what's left out. In short, how the information is 'staged.'

Lightening struck
and I was forced to get off
the train in Delft. Ewoud met me
and we drove the remaining distance
to Schiedam. Stepping out of his car onto
the quay, I witnessed an amusing performance.
Up ahead, in the slouching mid-morning sun, a man
clad in a navy-blue double-breasted brass-buttoned blazer
was dangling from a drawbridge—the counterweight needed
to open the bridge. His identically clad and slightly
more corpulent companion on the other side
had undoubtedly performed the same
maneuver just moments earlier.
The bridge yawned and
the idling schooner
slid through.

'His blazer is totally at odds with what's going on,' says Ewoud, responding to my enthusiasm for the scene. And it occurs to me that the little episode we just witnessed outside his studio is an accurate representation of the mechanism—and I use this noun because it suggests the verb 'activate'—that makes much of TRAAST + GRUSON's work so effective and so memorable.
     Taken to the extreme or experienced in an incongruous setting—think of the blue-jacketed men at the drawbridge or Magritte's pipe—clichés invite speculation and evoke a sense of t h e   m a r v e l o u s
     that most prized quality of all experience,
     to quote the art critic Robert Hughes.
TRAAST + GRUSON use clichés as thought instruments. The mechanism they employ is memory, triggered by cliché.

Tentoonstelling
schooltas
12e HEMA Ontwerpwedstrijd 1998/1999

The world of reality has its limits; the world
of imagination is boundless.

B o u n d l e s s n e s s .
The illusion of infinity. In Holland, this is known as het
Droste-effect.

Droste is both a quality cocoa and a chocolate manufacturer that has been in business for well over a hundred years. Its
red tins of cocoa still bear the illustration, created in 1900, of a
traditionally attired Dutch nurse holding a tray with the same red
tin of cocoa on it, which bears the same illustration, which bears
the same illustration, and so on, into infinity. At the time the image was conceived,
cocaine was present in cocoa. Hailed as a miracle drug that 'could make the coward brave, the silent eloquent, and render the
sufferer insensitive to pain,' cocaine was sold over the counter until 1916—one could even buy it at Harrods.
The nurse represented the healing powers of cocoa: a clichéd
image used to promote a cure-all. Today she stands for quality,
tradition and, emblematically, het Droste-effect.

1992. The assignment: a competition centered on the art of
exhibition design. The theme: het Droste-effect or the illusion of
infinity. Entrants are asked to translate the complex subject into
a readable and engaging concept. The Frans Hals Museum in
Haarlem agrees to host the winning exhibition.

But in the end, following the results of the competition,
the idea is scrapped. There will be no exhibition after all. The
reasons vary.
————Insufficient funds.
————A subject too complex for an exhibition aimed at the
general public.
————A jury lacking a solid basis on which to evaluate the
competition.
A valid point.
As a discipline, exhibition design is still too vague or ill-defined
to judge, at least in the conventional sense. It lacks a consistent
theoretical basis. And criticism, as we all know, is born of theory,
which arises from a historical context. Unlike its sister disciplines,
interior design and landscape architecture, exhibition design has
no such context. As a result, there is no consensus about what
makes it successful, sound, or even good.

That said, Marijke van der Wijst is widely considered
to be the best exhibition designer practicing in the Netherlands.
Her work, principally in service of the visual and applied arts,
is renowned for its distinctive subtlety and minimalist restraint
—unlike the work of TRAAST + GRUSON.

When I asked her to define exhibition design, she
responds by giving me a book: a handsomely illustrated monograph
entitled, simply, *Marijke van der Wijst* (1997).

'So often, graphic designers are brought in to create
exhibitions,' she says, 'when their realm—itself a very worthy
one—is the second dimension.'

Leafing through the book, I see that her well-reasoned and
beautiful work does help to define—by virtue of its quality and
quantity—exhibition design. Nevertheless, her relatively new book
proves my point: Without a consistent theory of exhibition design,
work done in the field continues to be judged largely according to
taste.

Het Droste-effect is predicated on the notion of repetition:
the unending cycle of birth and death, the steadily changing sea-
sons, the ebb and flow of ocean tides. It is indicative of Nature
and fundamental to the pattern of life. It makes way for the meas-
urable, predictable, continual, and certain: conditions inherent to

The architect Robert Venturi, speaking for himself and his
partner Denise Scott Brown, wrote: Two things we
love to acknowledge are the sublime ordinary
and the vital vulgar. TRAAST + GRUSON identify
with this statement.

our sense of security. Conversely, it makes way for the infinite
—for hope, desire, expectation, and eternity.

TRAAST + GRUSON take this train of thought as their point
of departure. Recurrent patterns and principles born of Nature and
of Mind are used to illustrate the interconnectedness of all things.
The space they envision depicts the infinite heavens above and
the finite world below. Mirrors are used to suggest the occurrence
of endless repetition in both realms. Short ladders reflect the
nature of human ambition—the sky's the limit—and the inaccessi-
bility of Nature's manifold secrets. The floor plan depicts a basket-
ball court. It suggests the playing field of life and, in my mind,
underscores the very human need for game playing as 'a means
of escape from the infinite, from the maze of this incalculable life,
from the burden and the mystery of the world,' to quote from
Pebbles on the Shore (1935) by J.M. Dent, who went on to talk
of 'a kingdom where justice reigns, where cause and effect follow
as the night the day, and where, come victory or come defeat, the
sky is always clear and the joy unsullied.' (Dent is referring here to chess, but of course

chess does resemble the game of life.)

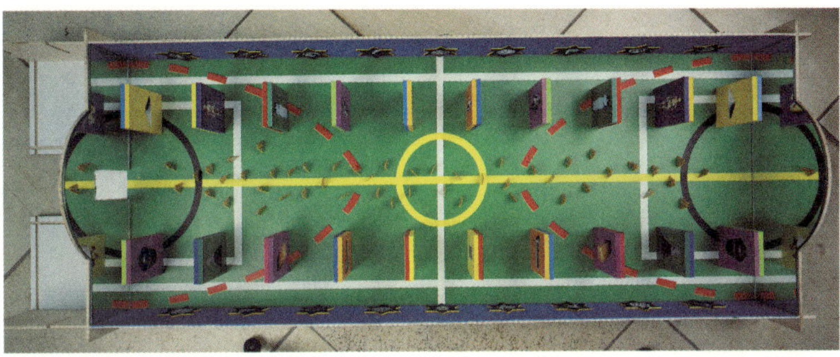

11

Marijke van der Wijst was on the jury appointed to select the win-
ner of this ultimately unsung competition. The jury rejected TRAAST
+ GRUSON's proposal on the grounds that it relied too heavily on
symbolism as a means of communication and failed to include suf-
ficient historical documentation. And yet the decision to construct
a visually oriented solution—appealing to the senses (gateway to the
mind)—is in keeping with het Droste-effect, which is, after all,
a visual phenomenon.

It is also very much in keeping with TRAAST + GRUSON's
manner of working.

'We're the first visitors to the shows we design,' says Edith.
*'So our first question is always the same: What would we like to
see?'*

'We use the technique of storytelling,' Ewoud says in turn,
*'to make sense of the material. Then we set about bringing the story
to life.'*

Storytelling involves a series of creative decisions.
Choices. The most important is point of view, a decision that colors
all others made in an attempt to get the story told. Point of view
defines the scope of the story, its 'angle of action.'

As designers, TRAAST + GRUSON are obliged to uphold the
client's point of view while, at the same time, developing their own
point of view relative to the material. They create, in effect, a story
within a story.

A good story always teaches us something. And even when
we may not think so initially, every story is about people. Who they
are. How they think. What they feel.

Land development. In the Netherlands this is practically an oxymoron. In a country with one of the highest population densities in the world, space is, quite literally, at a premium. Any undeveloped land lies beneath the surface of the sea. (As everyone knows, the Dutch are renowned 'landmakers,' having reclaimed vast areas from the sea to create polders.) The land that does exist is meticulously quartered and partitioned to accommodate diverse social and economic needs. From the very beginning, land use in the Netherlands has been, of necessity, puzzled out.

The year is 1991. The subject: plans for the redevelopment of an area north of Rotterdam known as Noordrand ('north rim'), a project initiated by the City of Rotterdam, the Department of Public Works, and Schiphol Corporation. (Schiphol is the country's principal airport and the owner of Zestienhoven, a municipal airport located in Noordrand.) The event: a public presentation of seven plans commissioned for the proposed redevelopment. Each of the seven plans—a year in the making—addresses the central question: What is the best way to integrate the various aspects of the desired development into the surrounding area? Each plan naturally purports to make the most of the available space while minimizing the impact the proposed building will have on the existing infrastructure and on the inhabitants of the area.

Clearly, in the minds of TRAAST + GRUSON, the event must be a platform not only for presenting the various proposals to the press and invited public, but also for demonstrating the efficacy of the plans submitted.

The effects of the proposed decisions had to be plain for all to see.

This is the key, the story within the story: to demonstrate, in an exacting and unambiguous way, the effect that each plan will have on the area, its surroundings, and the people living there.

'We also wanted to "break the ice,"' says Ewoud.

Inevitably, in situations where so many different interests are at stake—political, economic, social, environmental—policy makers are prone to favoritism. They have eyes only for their pet project.

Ewoud smiles.

P	U	
Z	Z	L
E	S	.

Nothing but child's play.

Or are they?

TRAAST + GRUSON translate Noordrand into an enormous topographic puzzle in the form of a table, the outline of which mimics the contours of the area. What's fixed is fixed (the railroad, for instance). Elements belonging to each of the seven plans are represented by large puzzle pieces that have been color-coded for ready identification. Participating policy makers and representatives of interest groups are invited to 'play' together—to assemble the various plans in an attempt to 'puzzle out' the best solution. Topographic maps detailing each plan are projected onto the surrounding walls. And, interestingly, the pattern on the rug underneath the table, purpose-woven for the event, represents Greater Rotterdam, of which Noordrand is but a part.

The project illustrates the importance of thinking not only about the material that informs an event or, as the case may be, an exposition, but also, and perhaps most especially, about the dynamics of the event. Who are the players? What's the score? What's at stake?

Monuments.

14

Marking time in space.
Marking space in time.

William I, also known as William the Silent (1533-84). Prince of Orange. Founder of the Dutch Republic. The monument marking his tomb is in the Nieuwe Kerk in Delft. The church and its illustrious tomb attract visitors from all over the world.

1995. Restoration of the venerated but timeworn monument is estimated to take at least five years. TRAAST + GRUSON are appointed the task of turning nothing into something—perhaps an even better explanation would be 'of getting people to look at nothing and see something.'

The famous monument is to be dismantled in stages. At a certain point, there will be virtually nothing to look at, with the exception of work equipment: ropes and pulleys and scaffolding and the like.

TRAAST + GRUSON's solution marks space as well as time. They erect a largely two-dimensional 'stained glass' representation of the monument, built to scale, in front of the space usually occupied by the famous memorial. (Nothing becomes something.) A high fence built in a similar 'stained glass' style extends off to either side, cordoning off the work area.

The 'stained glass' is functional as well as beautiful. When various parts of the monument are dismantled for restoration, clear glass, used initially to delineate the section while still intact, is replaced with colored glass. In this way, visitors can follow restoration activities. Similarly, the fence is comprised of information panels—which tell the story of William the Silent and provide information about the restoration project—and interchangeable transparent and opaque panels that can be used according to a worker's desire for privacy (behind 'closed doors,' away from the prying eyes of a curious public).

II.
ART OF CLICHÉ

We join Traast + Gruson's quest to invest familiar clichés with new meaning. The heart of the matter is stripped bare.

I first met Edith and Ewoud on the Fourth of July. Independence Day in America. A day rife with patriotic symbolism. Symbolism that has degenerated over the course of two centuries—the Declaration of Independence, a document that reads more or less like an indictment against the then King of England, was signed in 1776—for better or worse, into cliché. Across the United States, buildings and streets are festooned with Old Glory and images of Uncle Sam, a rather stoic, bearded Everyman clad in red, white, and blue. (He is, in fact, the Revolutionary War soldier Samuel Wilson. Wilson supplied meat to the U.S. Army in the War of 1812. The meat was stamped 'U.S.' and people said it stood for 'Uncle Sam' Wilson.)

I had no intention of celebrating the acclaimed national holiday. I see little sense in exercising cultural clichés while living abroad. Though people do. Here and elsewhere American expatriates stage picnics and barbecues as a salute to the country's hard-won freedom. As an attempt to uphold the nationalist cliché. Such celebrations were undoubtedly underway when Edith, Ewoud, and I met on American Independence Day in Schiedam, the Netherlands.

————Holland.

————Windmills.

————Wooden shoes.

————Tulips.

————Orange rounds of hard cheese.

A fistful of clichés, exploited to the nth degree in the name of commerce and Dutch national pride.

March 1993. The Annual Exhibition of New Issue Postage Stamps, commissioned by the Dutch Post Office (PTT) and hosted by the Jan van Eyck Academy in Maastricht. The PTT invited twelve designers, each representing a different member state of the European Community, to create a Dutch postage stamp.

What should a Dutch stamp look like?

Is it necessary to incorporate a Dutch motif or visual cliché into the design to make it Dutch?

Or is the appearance of the word Nederland qualification enough?

What about the influences of Dutch design culture abroad?

TRAAST + GRUSON addressed these and related questions in their design of the exhibition. They transformed the space into a referential all-Dutch scenescape teeming with visual clichés.

An expanse of green polder stretches beneath a blue sky spotted with rectangular white clouds. A green carpet resembles a sheet of stamps, which resembles the Dutch landscape as seen from above: strictly apportioned plots of land outlined by narrow bands of water. Residential areas are considerably smaller, often tiny. In Holland space is, quite literally, a state of mind.

> We have a lovely garden,
> a Dutch friend tells me.
> A postage stamp, but a garden nonetheless.

Turning a tired cliché on its head, TRAAST + GRUSON produced twelve promotional posters using the image of a historic windmill poised in a picturesque and decidedly Dutch landscape. Only one poster read 'Holland.' The remaining eleven displayed the names of the other EC member states.

The exercise is an interesting one. Clichés are effective because they represent predisposed thought and conclusion. (Everyone knows this image *belongs* to Holland!) Clichés are sound communicative devices because they are *unmistakable*. Misplaced or misconstrued, a cliché is no longer a declarative statement but a question. In this case, an appellation like 'France,' 'Italy,' or 'Spain' strips the image of its universal meaning. This isn't Holland—it's Germany?

Predictably, the commissioned designs reference Dutch themes and personalities.

'The Spanish designer,' Ewoud tells me, 'created an abstract design using the red, white, and blue of the Dutch flag. It had a Spanish flair but I wondered, Why not a flamenco dancer?'

Indeed.

DENMARK
BELGIUM
ENGLAND
GERMANY

ITALY
PORTUGAL
HOLLAND
FRANCE
NEDERLAND
NEDERLAND
NEDERLAND
80
65
80

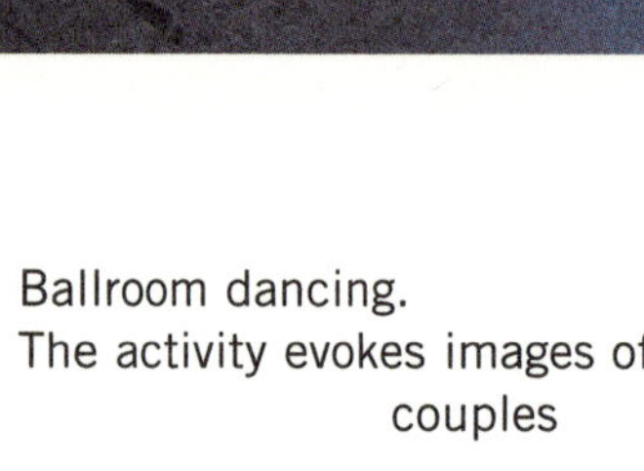

Ballroom dancing.
The activity evokes images of
      couples

              r o m a n c e
       love.

A red heart
    tells the story of
       love
            r o m a n c e
     couples
(ballroom dancing)
        cuddling

           cooing.
               It is
precisely this aspect of a weekend-long ballroom-dancing event
that TRAAST + GRUSON choose to emphasize—*the time when young
lovers steal away from the watchful eyes of their elders to cuddle and
coo in the privacy of an emerald garden...*
    1990. De Doelen Music Theater in Rotterdam.
TRAAST + GRUSON are asked to design the upstairs foyer. A long row
of plate-glass windows, overlooking the street scene below, accen-
tuates the length of the space, while the overt presence of the
supporting columns divides the area, more optically than otherwise, into equally spaced parts. A magnificent sixties-style glass
chandelier illuminates each part.

i s l a n d s
o f
i n t i m a c y .

Large, red, heart-shaped rugs mark the spot. Magenta filters color and soften the light from the chandeliers. Tall potted pines... these are props that De Doelen rents for every event.

Ewoud says, '*We wanted to rent twice as many, or more...*'

'*Implied privacy is no privacy,*' Edith interjects.

'*...to encircle each of the islands,*' he continues, '*but there was no money for it.*'

(Given the single-mindedness of lovers and the size of De Doelen, there was undoubtedly no lack of privacy during the weekend-long event. My guess, though, is that the 'islands' were occupied predominantly by couples for whom cuddling and cooing are activities associated with a very distant past.)

'*It was unforgettable, but I forgot about it anyway,*' Ewoud muses, momentarily lost in reverie.

Memories fade. Time eclipses even our finest hours.

Some things are worth forgetting—sensitive and embarrassing moments, mostly—but these memories are etched so deeply into the fiber of our consciousness there's no escaping them.

Like the exhibition featuring the results of a sculpture competition hosted by the Maas River commission. TRAAST + GRUSON built an aquarium—tall, long, narrow, replete with fish—and positioned the winning design and the four runners-up behind this tank. They mounted the designs on pedestals, making sure that the winning design stood taller than the rest, clearly visible above the water line.

'*It was the day before the opening. Everything was set. I mounted the stairs to survey the exhibition and just as my eyes cleared the floor and caught sight of the aquarium,*' Ewoud says, '*It burst. Water everywhere.*'

Still thankful that it didn't happen on the opening day, he admits that last-minute changes all but destroyed the original concept.

'*We have insurance now,*' he says with a wry smile.

The play on emotion is vital to the success of visual communications. The me-orientation tops the list—though the secondary *we, us*, and *them* are influential advocates as well. Emotion engenders a sense of connectedness. This, in turn, precipitates personal responses based on belief, attitude, aspiration. *I believe this... I think that... I desire...* Visual communications attempts to fill in the dotted line and to invoke a positive response to that which is being communicated.

I believe...

there's

no place

like home.

1999. An exposition of audiovisual equipment produced and marketed by Bang & Olufsen, commissioned by the trailblazing Dutch group Droog Design. Venue: Milan's annual fair featuring new consumer products.

TRAAST + GRUSON's design is exquisitely simple and, in its simplicity, remarkably sophisticated, thus reflecting the hallmarks of Bang & Olufsen's consumer electronics. A delicate metal framework creates the three-dimensional outline of an apartment in the dimly lit space (beautifully named 'Spazio Consolo'). Painted phosphorescent green, the tenuous structure is illuminated with black light. The only furniture is Bang & Olufsen—intercoms, television consoles, stereo equipment—all of it spotlighted. Motion sensors detect visitors in the space and trip the equipment on, revealing the identity of the

various rooms. Images of a flickering fireplace and the festive sound of chattering guests emerge from a television console in the living room. Romantic music defines the master bedroom, while a thrumming pop beat suggests space occupied by a teenager. And so on.

Bang & Olufsen's reputation is predicated on its technical superiority and sleek, no-nonsense design. While both factors are adequately represented by TRAAST + GRUSON's concept, what they believe truly sets Bang & Olufsen apart from the competition is pride of ownership. Associating the equipment with memories of hearth and home is aimed at conveying a sense of well-being.

1987. How long ago it seems, from the vantage point of the 21st century. So much of what characterized the eighties has lapsed into cliché: Sony's Walkman, Pac-Man, Sky TV, Solidarity, *glasnost*, 'We Are the World,' Halley's Comet, Blue Velvet, The Satanic Verses.

In Holland, the furor surrounding new legislation targeting public support for visual artists has dwindled, since that fated year, into a faint memory. At the time, however, people were up in arms. In an effort to assuage artists within its jurisdiction, the city of Rotterdam hosted a forum for discussing and debating the pros and cons of the new legislation. A panel of eight experts—policy makers, cultural historians, artists, critics, and curators—led the discussion.

In one of their earliest assignments, TRAAST + GRUSON designed what in many respects can be thought of as a kinetic sculpture. Eight brightly colored swivel chairs with exaggeratedly high backs form the decor. The stage is dark. Only the chairs and the experts seated in them are illuminated. The event is, quite literally, staged. Members of the audience take their seats. On the podium is a long table with what looks like tall, dark-brown panels extending upward behind it (the monochromatic backs of the eight chairs). The program begins when the experts swivel forward to face the audience. The multicolored chairs enliven the scene, pivoting from side to side as the experts debate the issues. The chairs also register agitation. (Presumably, sitting still and remaining poker faced in a swivel chair with a back that seems to rise to the ceiling takes a considerable amount of effort and concentration.) The design caricatures a whole host of clichés.

N o
f a d i n g
i n t o
t h e
w o o d -
w o r k
t o n i g h t.

Vignette.
In grim weather we pull up behind the slaugh-
terhouse. The parking lot is desolate, with the
exception of a pig's foot haplessly discarded on
the rain-soaked tarmac. We enter the building.
The director's office is small and compact. So
is he. The place is loaded with memorabilia
—photographs, certificates, pendants, plastic
figurines, fake flowers, toy cars, a large porcine
piggy bank. It smells of smoke and something
else I can't identify. Something acrid. He directs
us down the hall. 'Just keep going,' he says. We
do. It feels as if we're in a maze. Turning left,
we head straight until we turn again, continue
straight on, turn right, go straight again. We
follow the noise, which is becoming increasingly
sharper. We hear the sound of men's voices.
Water splashing. Steel against steel. Steel
against…bone. Thrack. Thrack. The narrow
corridor opens up into a great hall. Endless rows
of gutted pig carcasses hang suspended in
midair. Rows of white-aproned blood-splattered
butchers at work…

Hotel Central, 1991. Host to the famed and would-be-famous attendees of the Rotterdam Film Festival. The hotel's distinctively less famous but nevertheless well-frequented one-star restaurant, Le Muniche, is transformed for the week into a vegetarian eatery.

Aspects of well-known cinematic techniques seem to have informed the design conceived by TRAAST + GRUSON. Cinéma vérité: authentic and candid action. Fantasy film: fanciful departure from known realities. Film noir: sinister moods and bleak viewpoints.

The pig was cast in the starring role, adoringly elevated from foodstuff to ornament. Prefabricated padded walls, covered in red satin and quilted with gold spray-painted pig bones, were mounted over the tartan motif of the restaurant.

(In the textile industry, *abattre* refers to quilted or depressed effects in fabric.

It is French for 'to fell' and the root of the word *abattoir*. A surreal coincidence?)

A mock fruit bowl—the centerpiece—holds painted pig bones posing as bananas, apples, oranges.

The butcher that gave TRAAST + GRUSON the pig bones...

'Thigh bones,' says Ewoud, *'they're the right shape.'*

...reportedly slaughters 8,000 pigs a day. That's 40,000 pigs a week, 160,000 pigs a month... Before they could be painted and used as decoration, the bones had to be cooked thoroughly.

'It was sheer hell,' says Edith, twisting her nose in recollection of the stench.

Ewoud nods. *'Preparation for the event was the event.'*

festival restaurant
film festival
20th
rotterdam
Le Muniche
Central

'As plain as day,' Ewoud says matter-of-factly. Surveying the photographs of the exposition in question, we're compelled to agree.

Of course, Ewoud's comment could apply to any of TRAAST + GRUSON's projects. The two have an eye for the obvious, for something that those in pursuit of originality either become blind to or, worse, develop a deep distaste for. Many people feel that stating the obvious indicates a lack of imagination.

R o o s t e r s .

Fifty of them.

——————Identical.

————————————Long-legged.

——————————————————Stationary.

—————————————————————————————Each on an equal footing.

Only one, beneath a spotlight at the rear of the room, appears to be a cut above the rest. The star of the show.

The occasion: another HEMA-sponsored design competition. Entrants are asked to design an inexpensive, novel alarm clock. The winning design is to be produced and marketed by HEMA.

The year is 1996. The gothic and suggestively ecclesiastical space in Utrecht's Centraal Museum has been transformed into a pseudo-pastoral scene. Visitors wander among stilted, bright-colored birds sporting 'designer' alarm clocks and tags with the names and specifications of their creators. (Did any of the clocks mimic the sound of the rooster's familiar cock-a-doodle-doo, I wonder? Would that my alarm clock mimicked a bird rather than sounding a sharply unsympathetic bleep at the appointed hour.)

The starting point is obvious: A cock's crow is universally recognized as Nature's alarm clock. It's a cliché.

A way in.

Everyone gets it.

But there's more.

Repetition (remember, there are fifty birds) and exaggeration—almost to the point of overkill—liberate the cliché from its place among the ordinary. The effect is curiously surreal.

And that's the point.

Not surrealism.

Liberation.

III.
PERCEPTION

We look at the deliberately obvious and contrastingly subtle ways in which Traast + Gruson manipulate the scene to reinvigorate the seen. Everywhere we look, we see pieces of ourselves.

Expositions and staged events are explicitly artificial environments created to accommodate a certain idea or set of ideas centered on a specific subject, singular or plural. They have nothing to do with reality, which is always on the move, continually in the making.

'It's absurd to think,' Edith says, 'that we can recreate the past.'

And yet the past is often restaged. Case in point: the Rembrandt House in Amsterdam. The artist's atelier is presented as if it were the 'real' thing, as if Rembrandt has stepped out and will be returning at any moment. It's pure theater.

TRAAST + GRUSON were offered the project, but they declined.

'We like to call a spade a spade,' Ewoud says matter-of-factly. 'We're not interested in creating something that pretends to be what it is not.'

{ And I'm reminded of a place in Marfa, Texas, called the Block, home to the late conceptual artist Donald Judd. Obviously things have been tidied up since his death in 1994, and much of the living space, such as the bedroom and kitchen, is cordoned off. But the suggestion is made, nevertheless, that things are as he left them. I found it eerie and a little ridiculous (such is our lust for heroes). It made me think of another residence-cum-museum located in the Santa Monica Mountains in Los Angeles, California, a sprawling ranch that once belonged to America's favorite humorist cowpoke, Will Rogers (1879-1935). Today it's a historic state park. The residence is designed to convey things as they once were: 'After a cook-out on the patio and warm bantering with relatives and friends, Will and Betty Rogers would retreat to their private quarters upstairs to the rustic and much celebrated room known as 'Will Rogers' Den.' Betty had a nook in the adjacent bedroom where she would manage family business affairs, read or sew while Will…' }

Pure theater. But,
then again,
that's Hollywood.

The year is 1998, and the time has come for Bram Peper to say goodbye to his constituency. Having served as Rotterdam's mayor for seventeen years, he is moving on (and up). The State has appointed him Minister of the Interior. In a manner worthy of officialdom, the farewell event is characterized by pomp and circumstance. The guest list runs the gamut from notable personalities to minor players, all of whom held roles of greater or lesser significance at some point during Peper's mayoralty.

The event is staged in the upstairs foyer of De Doelen Music Theater in Rotterdam. Load-bearing columns divide the long, narrow space into equal parts. Using the architecture as a starting point—and bearing in mind that it is customary to shake hands when bidding farewell—TRAAST + GRUSON created a

p r o c e s s i o n - c u m - t i m e l i n e - c u m - c h o r e o g r a p h y r e p l e t e   w i t h   c a s t   a n d   c u e   c a r d s . Well, almost.

Following the repetitive spatial divisions articulated by the architecture of the foyer, TRAAST + GRUSON created a series of 'rooms,' each identical to the next in terms of layout and color scheme: maroon and gold, a staid—and therefore stately?—combination.

What distinguished each space was the year it represented. The first room was devoted to Peper's first year in office, the second to his second year, and so on. Each guest was 'cast' into the room marked with the year —and its events and political 'incidents'—to which he or she was most closely identified. Text also helped to contextualize the space. Three quotations in each room bore a direct link to the year in question: a remark attributed to Peper himself, a relevant press statement, and a citation referencing public opinion at the time. The rooms offered an informal setting in which the guest of honor could shake hands with—and bid farewell to—his constituency.

TRAAST + GRUSON's design provided Peper with a veritable trip down memory lane and, in a manner of speaking, also helped him save face. Moving through the years, prompted by the corresponding cast of characters and the trio of quotations, Peper did not have to concern himself with the fickle failings of memory (seventeen years is a long time).

The show, it seems, came off without a hitch—
       preserving
              public
                      perception of
                             Peper's
                                    political
                                          persona.

But reality, as I've said, is always on the move. And sometimes it just plain catches up with us. Even as he basked in glory, Bram Peper was destined to step down from his post as Minister of the Interior following allegations that he misappropriated city funds during his tenure as mayor of Rotterdam.

It is perhaps interesting to note that caterers hired by De Doelen to work the event had to be indoctrinated, as it were. It was up to Edith and Ewoud to rouse enthusiasm for their plan. Linens and flowers provided by the caterers had to match the selected maroon and gold color scheme. The importance of a coordinated image was not immediately clear to the caterers, whose business is not design but food service (set up—serve—clean up—break down). Clearly, lack of cooperation on their part would undermine the overall effectiveness of the design and spoil the cohesive nature of the event. (Theatrics demands unity—all players on the same team!) The event was chronicled a success. Being a space monger, De Doelen was keen to get hold of Edith and Ewoud's 'formula.' Understandably, the two denied the request. Design is, after all, a patterned response to a particular question arising from a particular need. While Edith and Ewoud acknowledge that design, like almost everything else, is a commodity, they refuse to think of their work as something that can be franchised. No McDesign for TRAAST + GRUSON.

How we see reflects who we are. (You know the adage: The glass is either half full or half empty.)
And who we are—shaped by such attributes as background, training,
mindset, proclivity, prejudice—influences how we see.
Similarly,
how we see ourselves
in relation to
the city
{ perceived only over the course of long periods of time }
colors our response. Where a real estate developer sees potential,
an environmentalist sees hazard; and where an architect sees
opportunity for renewed centrality, an urban dweller living on the
fringe sees the usual debris.

In order to get young architects to look at (to really see), think
about, and actively address issues related to urbanization—most
notably, housing—ten European countries initiated and now host a
biennial competition entitled Europan ('pan' stands for Programme d'Architecture Nouvelle).
The impetus is to inspire collective thought and to help generate
viable responses to concerns related to urban architecture, such
as wastelands; neighborhoods severed by highways; new residential
developments that have failed, for reasons not entirely clear, to
attract the necessary cultural, culinary and entertainment facilities
to bring the area to life; historical preservation; redevelopment;
mobility; and infrastructure. Unlike other competitions, Europan
actively involves civic officials and city planners so that winning
designs stand a good chance of being realized.

The year is 1994. The theme of Europan 3 is 'At Home in
the City.' Over 2000 architectural teams grapple with the problem
of creating homes for urbanites.

The NAi (Netherlands Architecture Institute) is to host an
exposition of forty-four award-winning projects and forty-one honorable mentions, each of which targets one of fifty-two selected
European cities. All entries have been conceived within the context
of one of eight predetermined themes: living in a historic environment, living beside parkland and water, rehabilitation of old
neighborhoods, reinvigorating the city center, redevelopment
of abandoned sights, bolstering and improving postwar neighborhoods, living on the border between city and countryside, and
living beside railroads, highways, and thoroughfares.

A complex proposition.
Enter: TRAAST + GRUSON.
They began by thinking about
cities—areas—neighborhoods—property.
Concepts
framed by boundaries—
defined by them—
contained by them.
This neighborhood runs north along the river.
That's a seedy area.
This city's hard to leave.

BAR

And thinking about boundaries led them to think about borders. How they're perceived, experienced, maintained, respected, crossed, violated. Borders between public and private space, for instance, are often nebulous.

'People think of McDonald's as a public space,' says Edith, *'but you can't go in there and eat the ham sandwich you made at home. There are very few public spaces that aren't defined by rules. And rules are borders, too. Park here. Dance there. Stop. Go. Do not enter,'* she says, using her hands for emphasis.

I'm reminded of a sign still displayed in the odd diner in America: No shoes, no service.

'Cities are over-planned,' says Ewoud. *'Every piece of ground has its designated function: residential, commercial, industri-al, recreational, scenic. It's all accounted for.'*

Owing to the complexity of the assignment—and given their think-ing on the subject—TRAAST + GRUSON wanted to present the materi-al within a well-defined and explicitly ordered structure, delineated (appropriately) by borders. They took as their point of departure today's typically urbanized European city center, an often rather run down, slightly grubby place.

TRAAST + GRUSON's floor plan has, at its heart, an empty gutter-rimmed traffic circle, replete with discarded needles sug-gesting the now common urban junky, and a tall solitary neon sign-post in the middle with the word **B A R** glowing at the top. The traffic circle leads out into eight colorful and decidedly more engaging spaces representing the different themes. Doors, fences, and run-of-the-mill urban objects—shopping carts, garbage cans, traffic lights—create physical borders between these spaces. Here visitors acquaint themselves with the target locations and the themes with which they are associated. Encircling the outskirts of this makeshift city center, prize-winning maquettes and relevant documentation are on display. Still further afield, outside the imagined periphery, visitors can peruse plans and drawings belong-ing to the designs that received honorable mention.

Later,
during an open discussion
organized to assess the quality
of exhibition design in Holland,
TRAAST + GRUSON were invited
to speak publicly about
their design for Europan 3.
One audience member was
noticeably upset.
'Why are you so angry with
TRAAST + GRUSON*?'* queried the
moderator.
'They simply go too far,' was
the exasperated response.

If the respondent had said something more specific, such as, 'They went beyond the accepted bounds of what's considered ethical' (and even this requires further clarification if it is to be useful as criticism), perhaps the discussion—for TRAAST + GRUSON, at any rate—would have proved to be more constructive.

'It was all about taste,' says Edith, shrugging her shoulders.

And quality, as we all know, cannot be measured solely on the merits of taste.

TRAAST + GRUSON seek to expand the boundaries of perception by getting us to see in new ways. Little wonder their work is sometimes met with sharp criticism. *'We like things as they are,'* their critics seem to stammer.

The French painter Robert Delaunay (1885-1941) is noted to have said:

The eye is our highest sense,

the one that communicates most directly with our brain, our consciousness.

And what the eye cannot see, the imagination conjures, creating all mode and manner of symbolism and ceremony to give visual expression—what Delaunay called 'pictorial speech'—to things like h e a v e n ,   t h e   h u m a n   s o u l ,   d e a t h .

1999. The subject: The Tangible Emptiness. A curator of Het Museon, a science museum in The Hague, is completing a historical study on the ritual of death as interpreted and experienced by the Dutch for the past 2000 years. His scholarship is occasion for an exhibition intended for a general audience. The material is vast and complex, not to mention provocative.

TRAAST + GRUSON's design reflects the curatorial view that to fully appreciate the content of the show, a single tour of the space is not enough. (Death is not a reductive subject.) This is not to say that the exhibition is not well ordered. It is. There is just so much to look at and to absorb.

Visitors first encounter a black box, which houses the exhibition. On one side, larger-than-life photographs depict an

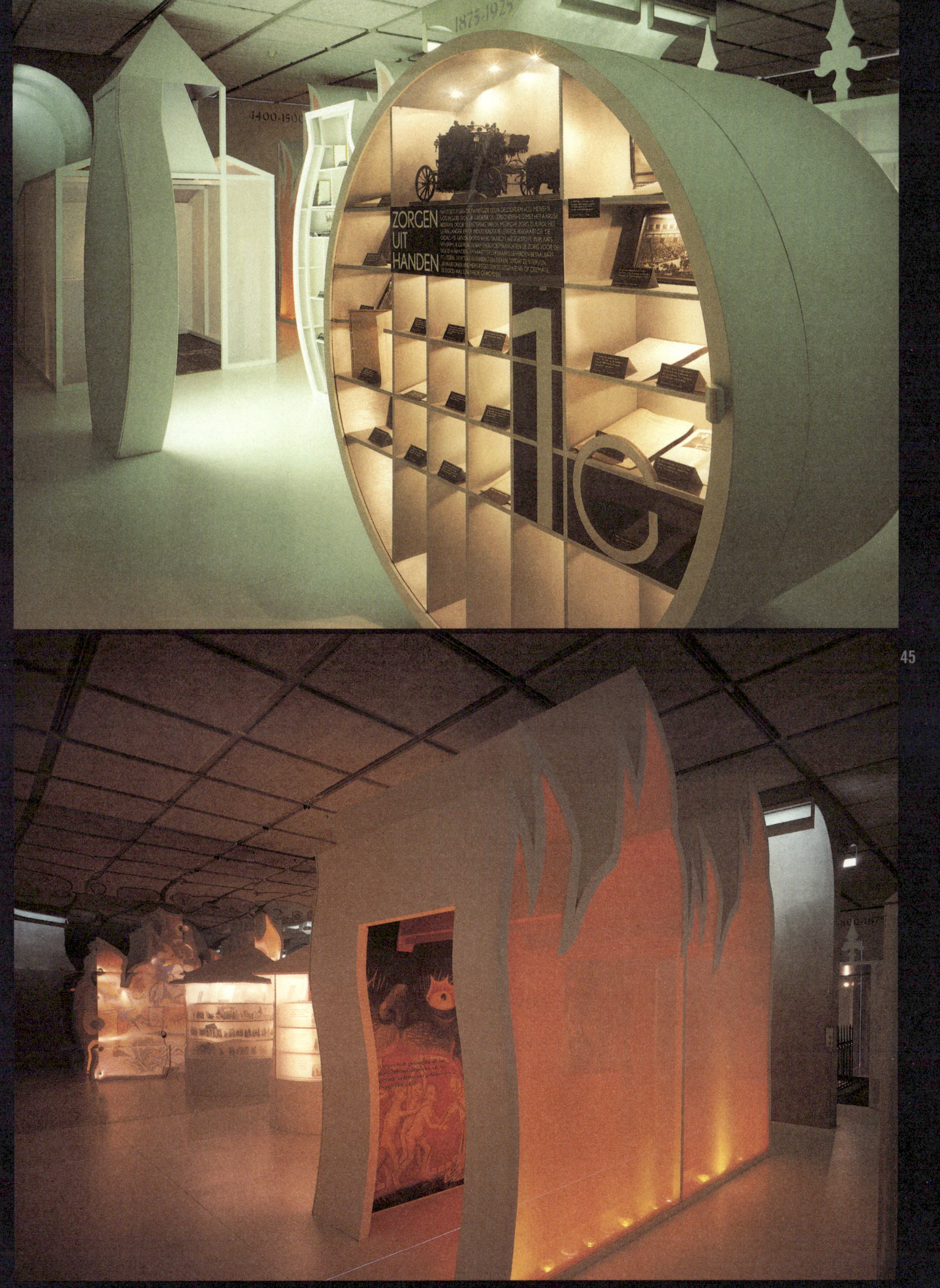

embracing couple. The woman's image fades. She's gone. The man embraces…the tangible emptiness.

This somber exterior is in stark contrast to the lively interior. A series of white mausoleum-like forms stand in the dimly lit space, each one a different shape—a tree, a church, a mosque, a flame, a coin, a carousel. These forms are endlessly multiplied in mirrors hung at opposite ends of the space. Visitors are reflected endlessly as well.

Allow me to digress here for a moment to say that the Latin word for mirror is speculum. Mirrors were once used to scan, or speculate, the movement of the stars. And stars, according to European folklore, represented living beings. Each person had his own star —bright or dull, depending on status and destiny—which was illuminated at birth and extinguished at death. Hence the expression 'born under a lucky star'—or an unlucky one, as the case may be.

The thrust of the exhibition is experiential. The white architectonic forms, which function as mini theaters, literally come to life when visitors approach, thanks to motion sensors housed in their construction. Given the highly symbolic and evocative nature of much of the material, text is kept to a minimum. It is largely left to the objects themselves—as mediators of meaning—to tell the vividly imagined, mythical, magical, mundane story of life's last subject, Death—

daughter
of
Night,
sister
of
Sleep.

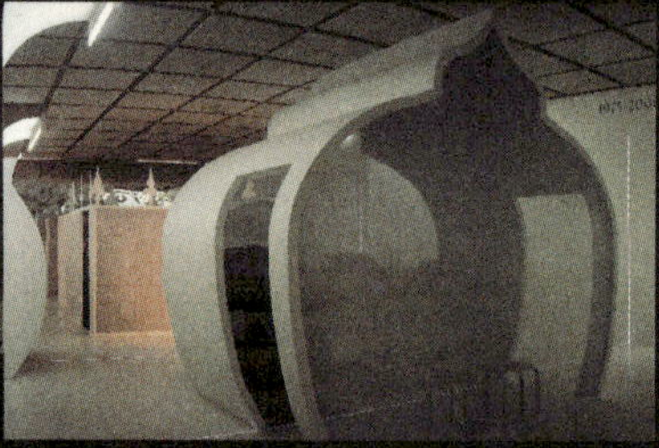

Outlined as a chronology, the story is told within the context of five key concepts: medieval representations, death as taboo, burial practices, death rites, and dirges.

'Visitors could select and play one of the top ten dirges,' says Ewoud, with a slightly mischievous grin.

It's true. A jukebox of sorts enabled visitors to play back recordings of the ten most popular funeral hymns. Those who criticized the show for resembling a circus should be reminded that even a circus is not free of death's pervasive power. Traditionally, a clown was the parodied image of a murdered king.

1975-2000
He

DEZE STEEN IS GELEGD
DOOR HARE MAJESTEIT
KONINGIN JULIANA
OP 9 MEI 1952 ALS BEGIN
VAN DE HERBOUW DEZER
KERK
VERBODEN
TE
ROKEN

Imaginings continue and the subject now is life—as perseverance, celebration, vision, unity. The year is 1995. The date recalls the p a s t—marking fifty years of freedom and prosperity following the German occupation of Holland during WWII. It marks the p r e s e n t—the city of Rotterdam is sponsoring five evenings of public debate on the subject of civic rebuilding and redevelopment over the coming five decades. And it marks the f u t u r e — Rotterdam 2045, fifty years hence.

The venue is the Laurenskerk (St. Laurens Church). The topic is the city. The initiative is meant to give policy makers and specialists representing different fields—politics, art and culture, science, education—as well as the general public, the opportunity to address important questions regarding the city's immediate and distant future. Providing a forum for discussion across the board, the city hopes to stimulate and encourage the various parties, each with its own reservations and interests, to work together in formulating plans for viable and sustainable civic development.

Each evening is designed to address a different set of issues: economic, social, structural, environmental, political. A specialist is invited to introduce the evening's program and to present ideas for further discussion and debate. Following a programmed interlude, the public is encouraged to participate in a round-table discussion.

Given the profoundly suggestive architecture of the church —with its altar, transept, nave, and chancel—TRAAST + GRUSON elected to 'paint' its forms with colored light, the predominant 'material' used in their design of the five evenings. By creating great volumes of color, they altered and transformed the space into a dramatic setting. The church was no longer a church. It was what TRAAST + GRUSON appointed it to be on any given night. Each event had its own unique environment.

The effect is reminiscent of the late Dan Flavin's ecclesiastical commission for the Santa Maria in Chiesa Rossa, Milan, in which the American minimalist combined pink, yellow, green, blue, and filtered ultraviolet lights to reinspire—if this is the right word—the interior of the church. The commission, one of Flavin's last (he died in 1996), *came from the parish priest who, believing that by restoring the church he could revitalize the surrounding neighborhood, asked the artist to light it.*

Using light and color, TRAAST + GRUSON effectively redefined the interior of the Laurenskerk—five times over. For instance, on the evening devoted to ecological and environmental issues, the massive pillars of the church were transformed into stately green trees, and the marble floors assumed a sun-dappled appearance. The round table was decked with camouflage cloth.

Rotterdam's multicultural community served as inspiration for the evening devoted to issues of social concern. Great bands of multicolored light merged, blended, and were separated in the tall space. (The effect must have been thrilling.) The corresponding round table was covered with a cloth bearing the symbol for yin-yang, which represents the fundamental cosmological principle that all things contain their opposite; for example, darkness is the absence of light.

A decidedly different effect was achieved on the evening devoted to economic issues. The interior was awash in warm golden light, and the floor was sprinkled with gold dust.

'We turned it into Uncle Dagobert's golden treasure,' says Edith.

I'm stumped by the reference, and say so.

Edith grins. 'You must know who Uncle Dagobert is,' she says teasingly.

I don't.

'He's Donald Duck's rich uncle. You know the character,' she insists.

And the top-hatted, smart-suited, spectacled old curmudgeon returns to mind.

'Oh,' I say, 'Americans call him $crooge McDuck!'

'All that dust,' Ewoud says reflectively. 'That floor still glitters.'

Perception is the same thing as thinking and knowing. It is often called information processing. We perceive the world with our senses—sight, hearing and balance, taste, touch, smell—and with our sense of time, direction, and motion. The philosopher William James believed that the deeper features of reality are found only in perceptual experience.

Indeed,
what we take in—and how we 'process' what we take in—determines how we see and experience the world.

Context is critical.

It is not surprising, then, that business and industry are so overtly concerned with public perception.

Seen in this light,
visual communications
is synonymous with
perception management.

Case in point: The ECT Mega-Effect, an exposition organized in honor of the company's first twenty-five years. ECT stands for Europe Combined Terminals. It is one of the largest container transshipment companies in the world.

The year is 1992. An enormous terminal—1500 meters square—located on the Maas River in Rotterdam is the designated location. Normally, the space functions as a fully automated car wash: standardized 20-foot-long shipping containers roll in dirty and roll out clean. For the purposes of the show, the space has been divided optically into a number of 20-foot-long parts. This has been done by stringing cable lengthwise and crosswise in the space, well above the heads of visitors but clearly visible. In this way, the measured circumference of a single container relative to many is always in view. Since there is only one actual container on display, this grid serves as a perceptual reference point. While visitors can imagine the approximate size of a standard container —having, on their way to the show, passed any number of trucks with containers riding piggyback—the grid provides context. Looking at the exhibited materials relative to one of the elongated forms drawn by the cables suspended above, the visitor can easily imagine the volume of goods that can be packed into a single container.

Echoing the geometry of the grid, the content of the show is divided into four sections. These represent the four modes of transportation: water, rail, road, air. It is within this context that the story of the international seaport is told, with special attention being paid to developments in the container transshipment business over the past twenty-five years.

The business is a late 1960s development. Since then, seaports have grown to gargantuan proportions, and the speed of cargo transportation worldwide has accelerated dramatically —thanks, in large part, to automated and computerized technology. (Read: job loss, a fact purposely omitted from this story.) In an effort to keep people in the picture, TRAAST + GRUSON projected huge slides—the size of a standard container— into the space. These slides depicted images of rugged seaport workers, for instance, drawn from ECT's archives. Anyone who visits an international seaport today will see that, while there's no shortage of activity, the place is almost devoid of human laborers.

As it turns out, the show—intended as a celebration to commemorate ECT's twenty-five year history and (presumably) the people

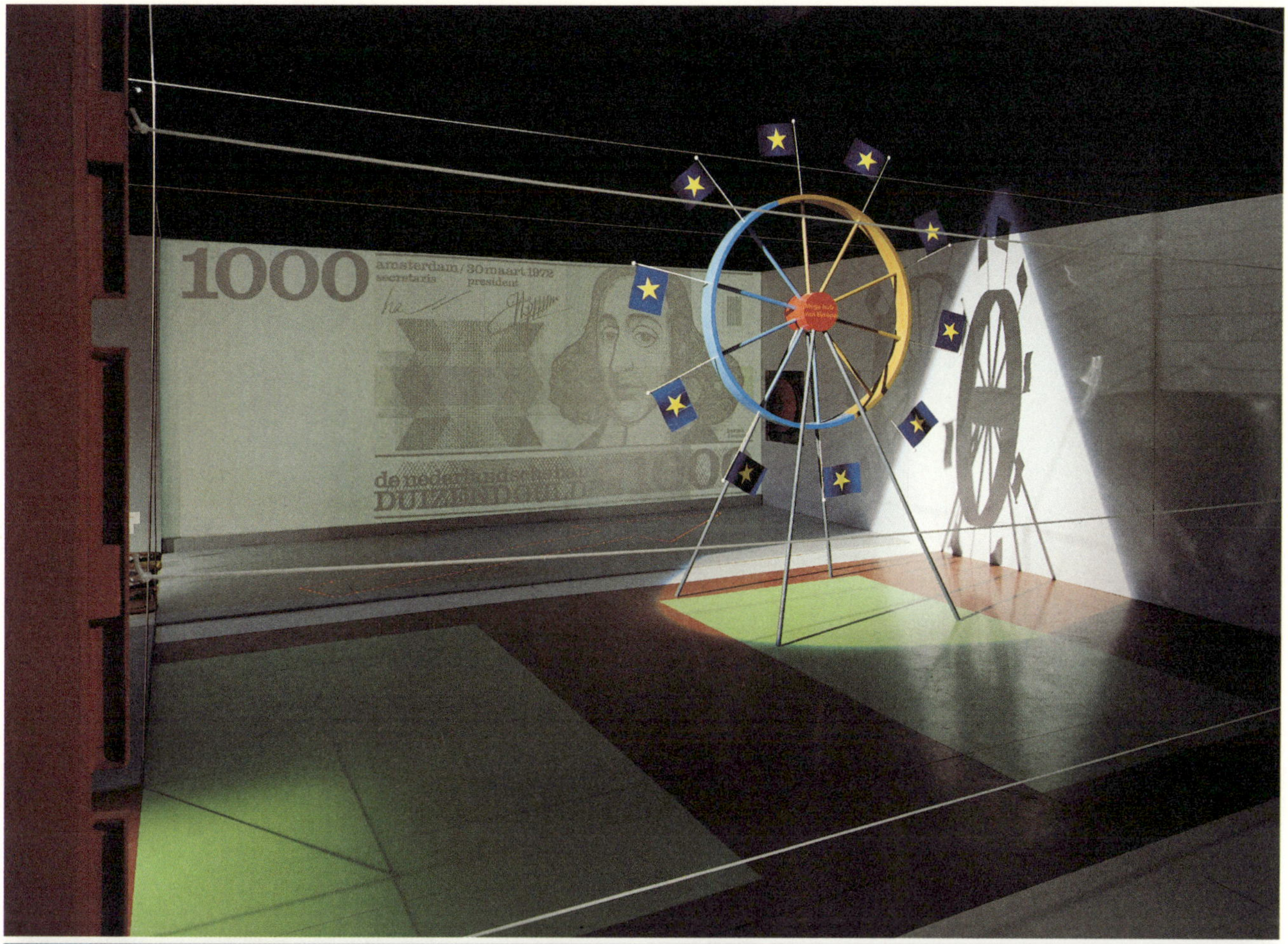
1000
amsterdam/ 30 maart 1972
secretaris
president

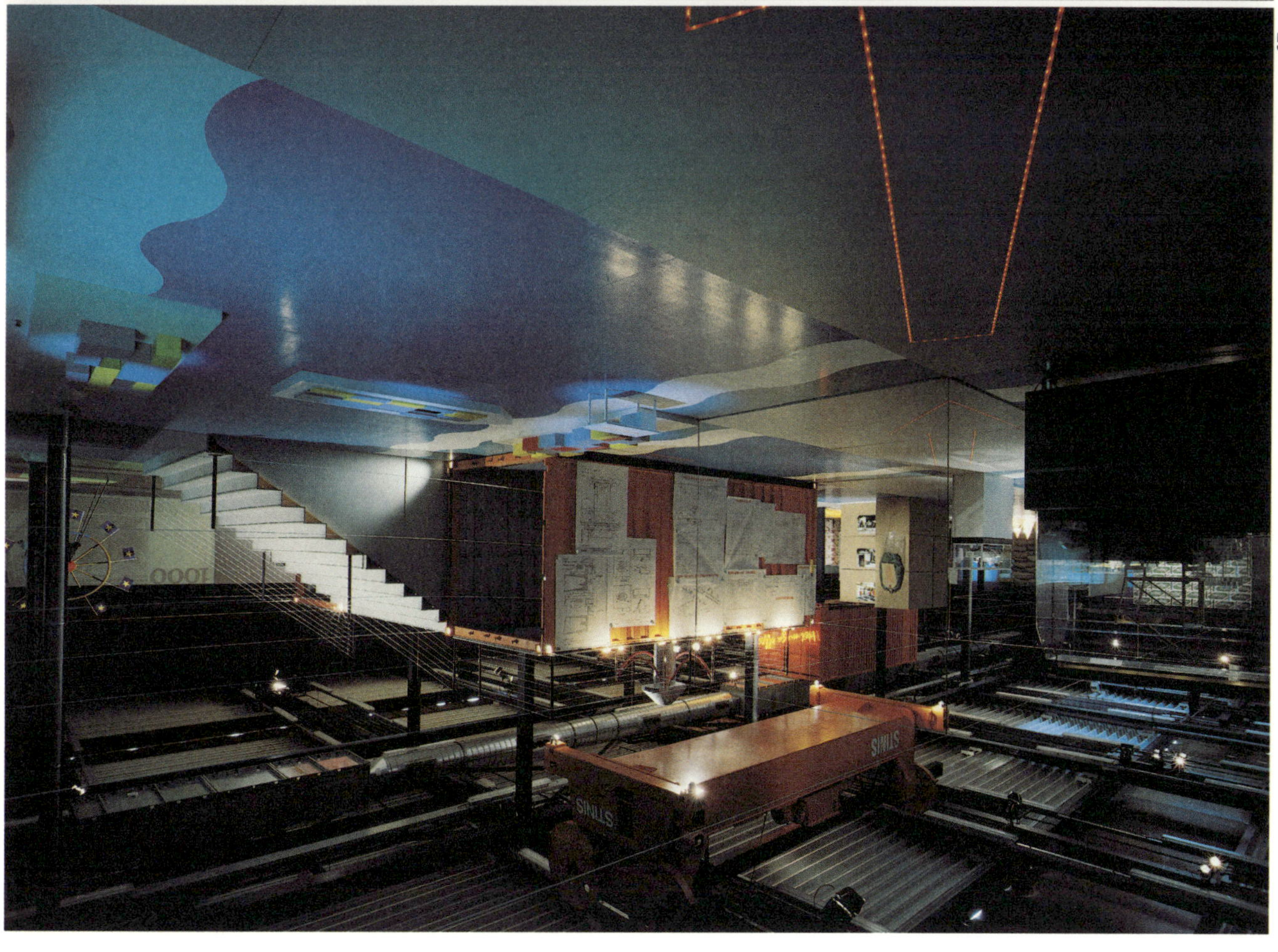

who helped make it a success—was only a pretext, or so it seems.
The show had a political aim. TRAAST + GRUSON's design actively
promoted the brawn, capacity, and streamlined efficiency of the
container transshipment business. ECT exploited the impressive
clarity of this message and used the exposition as a tool to lobby
in favor of the (dreaded) Betuwe railroad line which, when finished, will dissect the beloved 'green heart' of the Netherlands.
   Talk about perception management…

Design competitions are judged according to a shared set of assumptions and beliefs about what constitutes good design. A matter of perception.

The year is 1993. On display at the Frankfurt Book Fair are the 100 Best Book Designs from the Netherlands and Belgium, the two countries featured at this year's event. The books have been selected from hundreds of titles designed and published in the Netherlands and Belgium over the past six years. From the point of view of the jury, these are

The Best.

We do our best
to realize our best work,
to be considered
among the best in our field.

(As a child—according to my family who, in all the years since, have yet to let me live this down—I responded to polite queries about my day at school by stating, precociously, 'I'm the best in the class.')

In thinking about the assignment, TRAAST + GRUSON considered the fact that these 'winning' designs—these one hundred books—would be in competition with the thousands of books shown during the week-long event, not to mention the abundance of additional printed matter screaming for attention.

————Does the 'best,' then, constitute a design that is intrinsically strong enough to stand up to the competition?

————Is the 'best' something that rises to the top, like cream on milk?

————Does the 'best' supersede the 'mediocre' *of its own accord*, without being tagged the 'best'?

TRAAST + GRUSON's design represents a deliberate attempt to answer these questions.

Designers do their best
to realize their best work,
to be considered
among the best in their field.

A large, brightly lit, white space contains an array of low, three-dimensional, white forms—one hundred, to be exact—positioned in clusters. White walls, floor, and furniture are bedecked with an assortment of gaudily colored, run-of-the-mill logos, brand names, and clip art. Shadows are all but eliminated by the wash of white light. The space seems intent on imitating a two-dimensional plane.

N o t   a   b o o k   i s   i n   s i g h t .

The floor is patterned with the names of the winning designers. Each name is repeated to form a single black typographic line that wends its way from the entrance to a made-to-measure display case in which that particular designer's 'best' book is laid open for inspection. Some books undoubtedly hold up better than others in this surreal semiotic setting, but who's to judge which? Not to mention how and why?

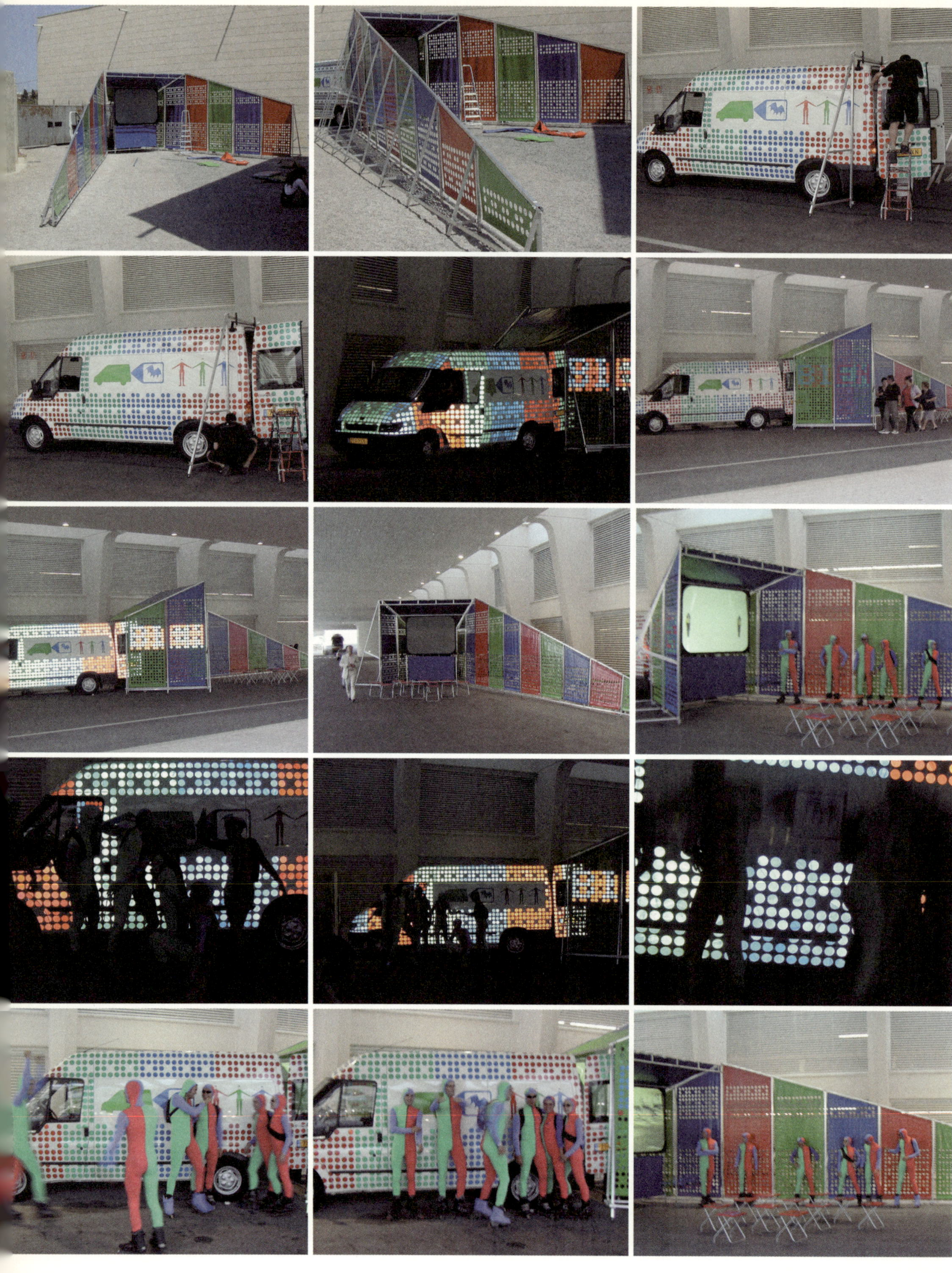

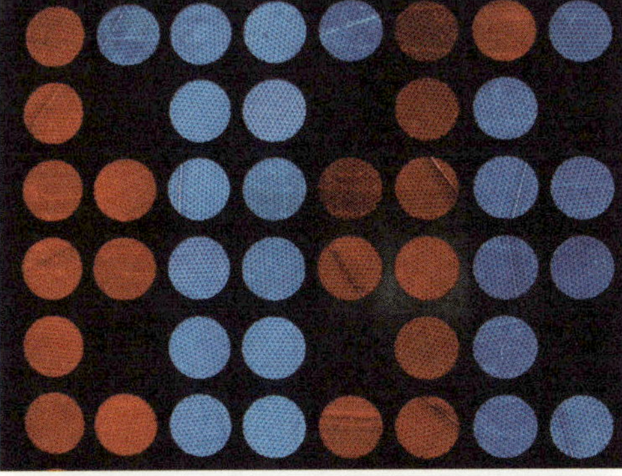

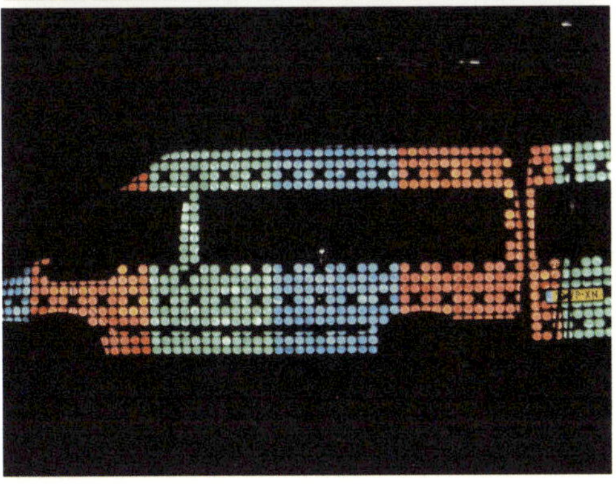

H u m a n   p a s s i o n s .

Uttered or silently lining a page like this one, words conjure up all manner of feeling and emotion.

Human passions.

Words sweep us onto another plane, if only for that fleeting flash of time in which the mind translates what the ear hears or the eye sees.

Human passions.

Apt theme for an art expo—Valencia's first.

The year is 2001. The occasion: the Valencia Biennial, curated by the Italian art critic Achille Bonito Oliva. The assignment: to design a mobile video theater, or VideoRom. The intention: to present three art videos at regular intervals throughout the biennial for random and spontaneous audiences gathered at various preselected locations around the city.

TRAAST + GRUSON rented a standard white truck and transformed it into a luminescent vehicle-cum-entertainment attraction, complete with color-coordinated, jump-suited 'town criers' on rollerblades. It would be up to these volunteers to verbally—and visually—promote the soon-to-be presented art video.

A tent of sorts was designed to fold easily into and out of the back of the truck, where the video monitor and playback machines were securely installed. Great care was taken to prohibit sunlight from reaching the screen and hampering visibility. Collapsible stools accommodated visitors wanting to sit down to watch the programmed video performance.

'We constructed it in such a way that curious onlookers and passersby could see what was going on without disturbing the audience,' says Ewoud.

No doubt the design attracted loads of attention. Reflective foil is impossible to miss. (Is a glowing vehicle a traffic hazard?)

While TRAAST + GRUSON feel that the project was well executed, they have their doubts about how well it functioned in practice.

'Planning events is different than curating a show,' says Edith.

Pity if the truck never made it out of the parking lot.

IV.
REPRESENTATION

We move through some of Traast + Gruson's characteristically straight-forward creations. There is more than meets the eye.

Plato suggested that we are trapped inside a cave and know the world only through the shadows it casts on the wall.

> The skull is our cave
> and mental representations
> are the shadows.

There are four major forms of representation: visual images, phonological representations, grammatical representations, and what cognitive scientist Steven Pinker calls 'mentalese.' Mentalese is the mind's lingua franca, with which we are able, in Pinker's words, to 'describe what we see, imagine what is described to us, carry out instructions, and so on.' In effect, mentalese is the facility that enables us to grasp the content or gist of something. Having grasped it, we can personalize whatever it is that has stimulated our attention. We relate it to what we already know, bringing into play other forms of mental representation. (For example: I sounded out the idea in my mind and visualized the possibilities before making some notes.) In short, mental representations and the processes they access embody human thought and action, and thus pave the way for the acquisition of new knowledge and experience.

It is this aspect of human cognition that dominated TRAAST + GRUSON's thinking when they designed a series of exhibitions for newly constructed theme rooms at the Centraal Museum in Utrecht. A concern for how the mind responds to what the eye sees broadened into a concern for how the eye can look at familiar things and be made to see them differently—and for how design can stimulate the mind to register and respond to such things in novel ways.

> Bright blue
> shadowless space
> transforms
> centuries-old paintings
> into luminous portals—
> the past becomes
> the present.

The year is 2000. The Centraal Museum is reopening its doors to the public following a massive renovation. It's a big event. Edith and Ewoud meander anonymously through the crowd.

'Good heavens!' Edith overhears a visitor exclaim, obviously shocked by the overwhelming blueness of the space in which paintings of townscapes, streetscapes, and interiors by seventeenth-century Dutch artists, including Pieter Jz. Saenredam of Utrecht, are on display. Walls, floor, ceiling—everything is blue. 'Imagine that the whole museum looked like this!'

('That's the point,' says Ewoud, referring to the event, 'the whole museum didn't look like that.')

The visitor and her companion refuse to consider the paintings in this context. To them, and reportedly to many others, the design is a complete abomination. The hubbub surrounding TRAAST + GRUSON's presentation resounds with 'How dare they!'

'What we were interested in,' says Edith, 'was the heightened visual effect resulting from the juxtaposition of complementary colors—in this case the coldness of blue, meticulously selected for its complementary properties, and the warmth of the richly colored, varnished canvases.'

HET UTRECHTSE STADSBEELD IN DE 17DE EEUW UTRECHT IN THE 17TH CENTURY

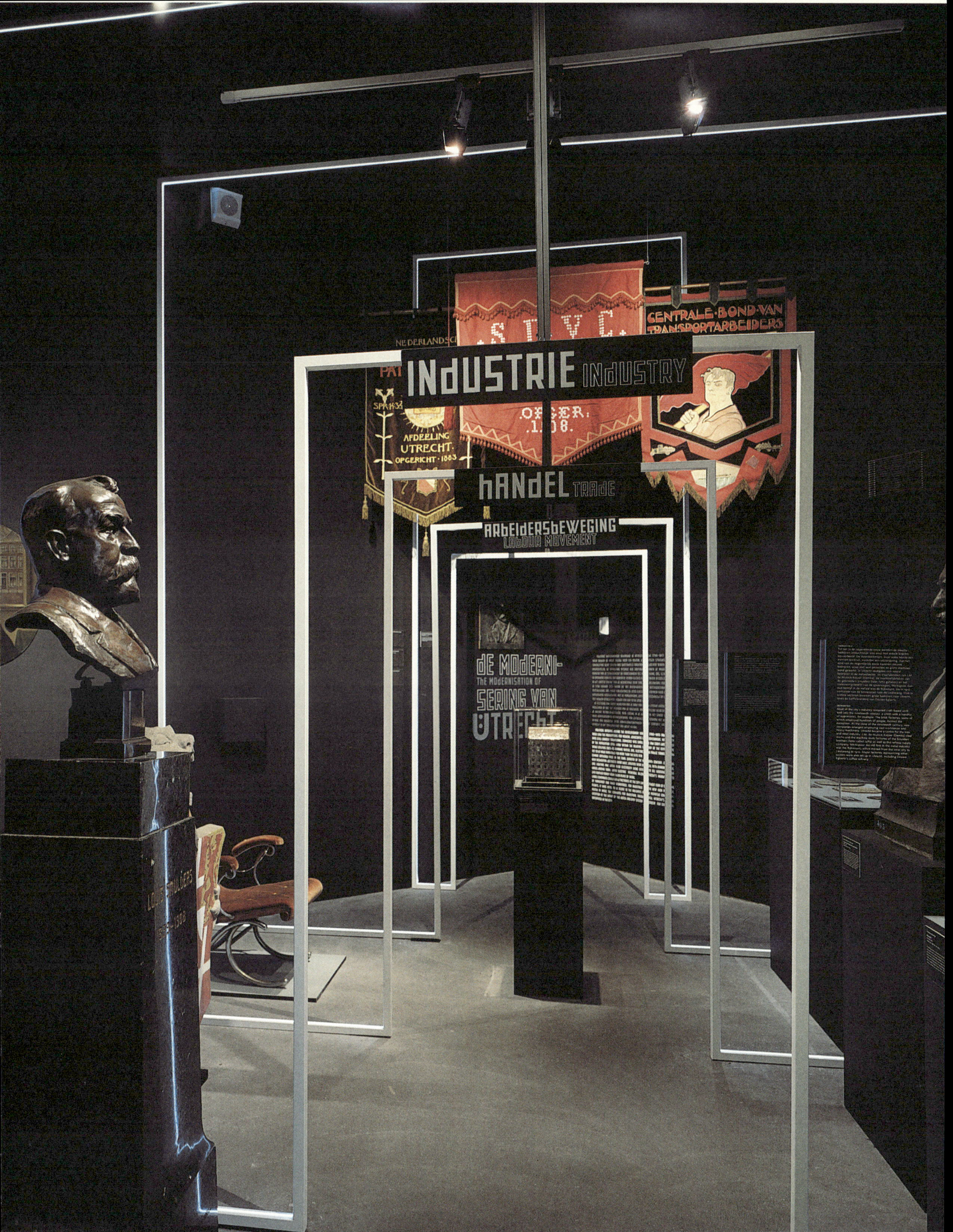

CENTRALE · BOND · VAN
TRANSPORTARBEIDERS
NEDERLANDSC
· S I V C ·
INDUSTRIE INDUSTRY
AFDEELING
UTRECHT
OPGERICHT · 1883
hANDEL TRADE
ARbEIDERSbEWEGING
LABOUR MOVEMENT
DE MODERNI-
THE MODERNISATION OF
SERING VAN
UTRECHT
LOUIS MULDERS

'The blue is so prevalent,' Ewoud continues, *'it's disorienting. The dimensions of the space are neutralized. Everything appears flattened. The only thing that remains,'* he says, eyes widening in remembrance, *'are the paintings.'*

TRAAST + GRUSON manipulate the experience of looking. In effect, the blue sets visitors up. They are forced to look at the paintings in a new light, so to speak. Or they are driven to dismiss the display out of hand for being in what they consider bad taste.

Janneke Wesseling, art critic for one of Holland's national daily newspapers, is among the latter.

'The idea of situating townscapes in a blue environment is totally absurd,' she reported. In her opinion, the paintings —and she referred specifically to the work by Saenredam —were ridiculously reduced to postage stamps destined to fade into nothingness. 'For the visitor,' she wrote, 'the only apparent conclusion is that the paintings are not worth looking at.'

Although museum director Sjarel Ex appreciated the designers' attempt, he concedes that the idea was not well executed. 'Last-minute changes didn't help matters,' he tells me.

TRAAST + GRUSON's idea for the space included propping up each painting on an easel—blue, of course—and positioning the easels within the space in a nonchalant manner, as if the paintings were works in progress. Objections were raised (understandably) when the paintings were brought out of storage for the installation. 'The paintings will be too vulnerable.' 'Visitors will bump into them.' 'If one of the easels topples over, the painting will be damaged.' 'There's too much of a security risk.' And so the paintings and the easels—with the exception of two securely riveted to the floor—were mounted on the walls.

The blue space, envisioned as a setting for paintings on freestanding easels facing this way and that (a playful idea), was reduced to a blue cell with works of art hung on the walls—on easels that, I imagine, must have seemed out of place. After all, an easel is meant to stand in space, not to be hung flat against a wall.

A second space featured a selection of 17th century portraits of Utrecht regents. Here again, TRAAST + GRUSON were interested in representing the paintings in a new way. Although this time the idea was to keep things as they were—in the past.

The reverence once paid to these regal subjects is mocked by the installation, which consists of a short flight of stairs leading to the wall where the paintings are hung. Broad treads are covered with rosy-red carpet fitted with brass rods. The steps are reminiscent of those leading to an altar. Personages represented in the paintings appear to be elevated above their already superior aristocratic station. It is not immediately clear that these portraits —in the eyes of TRAAST + GRUSON anyway—represent

t h e

t r a n s i e n c e

o f

f a m e .

The hollow sound of footsteps on the stairs undermines the credibility of the seen (read: scene) and seems to say: appearances do not always coincide with reality. Having mounted the hollow stairs, visitors find themselves face to face with portraits that have been reduced to little more than what one journalist called 'mug shots.'

'The idea for the theme rooms,' explains Sjarel Ex, 'was developed to provide an opportunity to create exhibitions representing various aspects of the broad-based and divergent collections found in this museum. Portraiture, seventeenth-century painting, Utrecht masters, sculpture, artifacts, applied arts, and much more.'

In addition to the blue space and the portrait room, TRAAST + GRUSON designed an exhibition devoted to Industry and Trade in Utrecht in the nineteenth century, and one featuring the famous Utrecht painter Abraham Bloemaert. In the latter, artifacts found by archeologists in the ground beneath Bloemaert's onetime residence are displayed in a circular, well-like cabinet specially built for the event. Many of the things on display are represented in the exhibited paintings. TRAAST + GRUSON once again play with time. The art mirrors the objects, and the objects mirror the art. In this way, the past becomes the present, and the present becomes the past. TRAAST + GRUSON's solution effectively brings the paintings (back) to life.

telefoon
GEMEENTE GIRO
INTRODUZIONE
NELLA STRADA
INTRODUCTION
THE STREET
COLOFONE
COLOPHON

  More than in the past, modern-day streetscapes are heavily
designed environments. Architecture, street furniture, storefronts,
signage, lighting, pavements, parks, and graffiti (designed to be
seen) all vie for attention. The Dutch have a longstanding tradition
of high-quality design in the public domain. Civic services are distinguished by original and, in some cases, award-winning house
styles and corporate identities. The previously state-owned Royal
PTT Netherlands and its subsidiaries, PTT Post (now Royal PTT Post) and
PTT Telecom (now the public company KPN Telecom), are classic examples of the
sophistication and durability of Dutch design.

   For over eighty years, the PTT has exercised a design
policy that includes the annual issuance of newly designed postage
stamps (frequently the result of design competitions that draw a great many entrants), printed matter,
interior architecture, signage, lettering, fashion, and street furni-
ture such as mailboxes and telephone booths. The result is a clearly recognizable and consistently evolving style, image, and identity.

PTT was a veritable brand, replete with values and personality,
long before the trend known in corporate circles as 'branding'
emerged in the late nineties.

1992. An exposition of PTT design throughout the decennia, entitled Signs in the Street. The occasion: the Trienniale di
Milano, an international design show. The idea: history is an
amalgamation of intersections between the ever-in-the-making
present and the continuously appointed past.

The late Argentinean author, Jorge Luis Borges, wrote:

To see a thing one has to comprehend it.
An armchair presupposes the human body,
its joints and limbs;
a pair of scissors, the act of cutting.

TRAAST + GRUSON's design, like the items on display, is immediately
understood. A mailbox, for example, cannot be mistaken for

anything else; the design may vary but its visual lexicon is universal. They have built a theatrical set in which to present various key designs from the PTT archives—items ranging from the first public telephone in Holland to the more recently designed civic mailbox. A series of flats representing façades drawn from a typical Italian street scene are arranged to form an intersection. (The subject is Dutch design, but the venue is unmistakably Italian; the overall layout of the 1992 show is the work of Italian architect Aldo Rossi.) While one street is clearly old-fashioned—and therefore contains the older designs—the other is contemporary and thus fitted with the latest furniture and so forth. The design history of the PTT is played out, as it were, within this overtly staged setting.

Exhibitions are staged
events.
Events are staged, too.

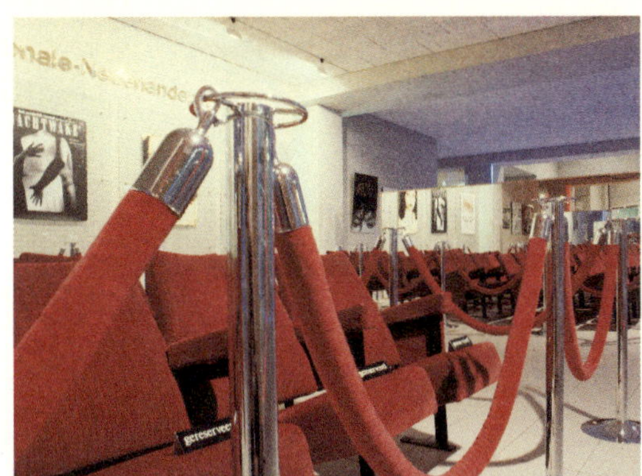

The year is 1989 and TRAAST + GRUSON are asked to design a décor for the lobby of the Rotterdam Schouwburg (playhouse), host to this year's National Theater Festival. The décor sets the tone for the week-long event, which features performances of the ten best plays by Dutch playwrights, and provides a platform for panel discussions held for the benefit of participating professionals and interested members of the general public.

Plays have been selected by members of the theatergoing public, who were asked in advance to vote for what they considered to be the best Dutch play.

'The best of anything exaggerates the importance of one thing to the exclusion of many other – no doubt equally commendable – things,' says Ewoud. 'We decided to make exaggeration our point of departure.'

Theatergoers arriving at the Schouwburg look puzzled. Rows of red velvet theater chairs are situated in the lobby. One hundred chairs to be exact, though there appear to be several times that number: mirrors flank the rows of chairs on either side, greatly exaggerating the scene/seen. The chairs are roped off, and each one bears a white sign that reads: Reserved.

The scene triggers an impromptu performance.

[People milling about]

'Do you suppose this is where the performance is being staged?'

[Looks of uncertainty]

'Where are our seats?'

[Relief]

'Good thing we made reservations.'

The platform for the panel, on the other hand, resembles a surrealist pantomime that could be titled *Tribute to René Magritte*. It consists of a long white table. Six chairs on one side face the audience. Suspended by an invisible thread above each chair is a top hat, which hangs well above the head of whoever sits there. A horde of microphones stands on the other side of the table (another exaggerated scene). Each mouthpiece is fitted with a red cover, making the mikes look like so many red clown noses.

Panel participants balk.

'Theater is serious business!' they seem to say. 'We will not be made fools of!'

'The festival director had his hands full,' says Ewoud. 'We practically had to supply him with a script to help him counter objections raised by participants put off by the theatricality of the scene.'

'It's like that scene in *Shadow of the Vampire* with Willem Dafoe,' says Edith. 'Dafoe's character says, "It's not a contract." Someone answers, "Why indeed it is, sir," to which he replies, "Oh, well, in that case I need some makeup. [Powder] Ah yes, I see. A very good contract!"'

She laughs. 'The participants couldn't see the humor and irony of the platform because they didn't have their makeup on.'

Equipping a client with a convincing argument to counter objections to a design—raised by the client's audience or associates—is a very real and important aspect of TRAAST + GRUSON's business. The flip side (there's always a flip side) occurs when a client's enthusiasm is so great that the design becomes something other than what it was intended to be.

Case in point: Who's Afraid of Ancient Blue? (an unmistakable and rather cheap play on the title of Barnett Newman's famous abstract expressionist painting, Who's Afraid of Red, Yellow, and Blue?).

The year is 1997. The occasion: an exhibition of Egyptian sarcophagi and Roman busts hosted by the Rijksmuseum van Oudheden (National Museum of Antiquities) in Leiden. The location: the Taffeh Gallery, a voluminous space built to house the remains of the Egyptian Temple of Taffah, permanently on display.

Objects featured in the exhibition stem from a period in which painting was subordinate to sculpture. Architecture was adorned with colorful mosaics and statuary richly decorated with colored paints. The largely monochromatic objects on display in Leiden bear little resemblance to what they looked like when they were created. Back then, Egyptians believed they lived under a gigantic blue tent held in place by four pillars positioned just beyond the visible horizon to the north, south, east, and west.

TRAAST + GRUSON's design reflects these ideas. An array of computer-directed colored lights reinvigorates the objects on display and returns them—suggestively—to their original colorful state. More lights are used to mimic daylight (when the sun is directly overhead and no shadows are cast) and darkness. The effect is dramatic, although some visitors may have difficulty dissociating the dancing lights from the seventies disco scene.

A huge blue tarpaulin suspended from, and not far below, the ceiling recalls the Egyptians' belief that their isolated oasis was contained in a tent.

'The client loved the idea,' says Edith.

'A bit too much,' adds Ewoud, scowling.

'The show was christened "Who's Afraid of Ancient Blue?" and the next thing we knew, there were blue invitations, blue napkins, blue umbrellas, blue everything.'

'I still have one of those blue umbrellas in the trunk of my car,' says Ewoud, his grimace easing into a smile.

The public didn't seem to object to the title. The show, which was open for two years while other areas of the museum were undergoing renovation (the reason why the different objects in this show were brought together in the first place), was reportedly very well attended.

More than anything else, exhibition design is about emotion. The design—which can be viewed as a vehicle of content—has to appeal to a visitor's senses. This engagement serves to liberate visitors from the here and now. It releases them from the realm of the known and transports them into a world composed of new impressions and experiences, which they then come to call their own. What makes an exhibition memorable is the quality of feeling associated with having seen and experienced the show, in addition to the clarity of the message the show was designed to convey.

A space may be designed to represent a garden, but what makes it a garden is not only the fact that it looks like a garden but also that it feels like a garden, because if it feels like a garden it will be used as if it actually is a garden.

1999. A historical palazzo called La Posteria is the site of a show featuring a project by Droog Design entitled *Couleur Locale*. Items on display include products created by Droog Design for the Oranienbaum Estate in Germany and glassware for Salviati. The occasion is the annual international design show in Milan.

TRAAST + GRUSON have created a faux seventeenth-century French garden with symmetrical hedges, a fountain, and a greenhouse. Certain designed objects are displayed on the hedges, which are three-dimensional forms covered with fake grass. Others are part of the garden furniture and include a sofa made of straw, a wicker chair, and a tree-trunk bench with copper backrests. Lighting designs illuminate the interior of the mock greenhouse. Glassware is displayed in the fountain, just above the surface of the water.

'It was uncanny,' says Ewoud. '*The texture of the glassware resembled the bubbling fountain. We had no idea!*'

(Serendipity is such a lovely phenomenon.)

For TRAAST + GRUSON, the design proved to be a success when, during a cocktail party hosted after public visiting hours, guests took their drinks and gathered around the fountain—as if the garden was a real garden.

Collection
Droog
Design

'a selection'

A real trading ship,
built in the year 1000, is the centerpiece of an exhibition entitled
1000 Jaar Markten in de Domstad (1000 Years of Markets in Cathedral City), hosted
by the Centraal Museum in Utrecht—also known as Cathedral City.
While Utrecht's current market, Vredenburg, is relatively young (it was
established in 1975), the city boasts an impressive history as an international market center.

The story begins at a time when Utrecht was still a small town accessible to big sailing ships. Merchants traveled there from England, Scandinavia, and Germany to trade their wares. As the city grew and prospered, land became scarce. City officials voted to silt up the Vecht River to make way for a growing population. The decision was disastrous for the city's markets. International supply and demand continued to increase, and the capacity of trading ships increased as well. The larger sailing vessels could no longer reach Utrecht, and its position as an important market center dwindled. Attempts in the seventeenth and eighteenth centuries to dig a canal that would reconnect the city to the sea failed. It was only in the second half of the nineteenth century that Utrecht was able to resume large-scale import and export activities, thanks to the coming of the railroad and the completion of an artificial waterway known as the Merwedekanaal.

The year is 2001. TRAAST + GRUSON's solution for the exhibition is highly graphic, almost logo-like. The design represents, in the broadest of terms, the evolution of the city, from its origin as a small trading town to the present day. Color indicates significant aspects of the changing topography of the city. For instance, waterways are represented by abstracted blue forms painted onto the gallery walls. In contrast to the minimalist setting, a fantastic variety of objects—not least of which the trading ship—are on display. Drawings, prints, paintings, relics, artifacts, tools, utensils, photographs, documents, and maquettes combine to tell the story of Utrecht.

'I liked TRAAST + GRUSON's idea for the design,' museum director Sjarel Ex tells me, 'and I liked how the rooms looked when the design was finished. However, as soon as the collections were moved in, it all went wrong. The concept was good, but the design and the works of art were a poor match.'

The public didn't seem to be bothered, however. According to the director, roughly four thousand history buffs visited the exhibition. Their chief concern was the curatorial accuracy of the show.

'Most of them, I'm sure, didn't even notice the design,' he adds.

SCHUIVEN MET MARKTEN
DE STAD ALS MARKTMEESTER
GEEN GOUDEN EE
VOOR UTREC

I am firmly convinced that certainty
lies not in finding new material
but in rearranging what already exists.
—Blaise Pascal

Design has everything to do with patterning. It brings together different source materials and rearranges them with the intention of creating something new. An ordinary object can have an extraordinary effect depending on how it's used and what it represents.

Brown collapsible cardboard boxes bring to mind the activity of moving from one house to another; we've all been there. Naked light bulbs are reminiscent of the period of time between moving in and settling in. A large collection of wineglasses suggests catering.

1989. TRAAST + GRUSON use these everyday objects—each one a strong visual symbol—in their design for a congress entitled De Kwaliteit van wonen in de jaren 90 (Housing Quality in the Nineties). The focus of the event is innovative solutions to urban planning and residential development in the Netherlands over the next ten years. The five-day congress is held in the main hall of what used to be the passenger terminal of the Holland America Line, the erstwhile cruise-ship company. The space is massive:

2500 square meters. Bringing the space down to a more human scale is the first priority. Second to this is the need to improve the acoustics.

To begin with, the designers divide the cavernous space into four sections. These divisions are in keeping with the architectural lines drawn by the four vaulted windows that describe the façade on the Maas River side of the building. Each of the four spaces has a specific function. Lectures are held in the congress area. There is a restaurant, a reception area, and a library-exhibition area. Walls built of brown boxes stacked like bricks (acrylic sealant is used as mortar) delineate each area. Given the relative size of the space, the effect is nothing short of monumental. The stacked boxes reach a height of nearly 12 meters.

Illuminated with fuchsia light, the wall in the congress area serves as a backdrop for the individual speakers, like curtains on a stage. The wall in the exhibition area is used to display

technical drawings, artists' renderings, and photographs of exceptional urban and residential developments selected by congress organizers. Naked colored light bulbs create a repetitive pattern on the wall denoting the reception area. These bulbs hang in the open spaces left by 'missing' boxes. The lights are programmed to flicker on and off at random. At night, when entertainment is provided, the visual rhythm of the lights appears to mimic the rhythm of the music. In the restaurant, every other box used to form the wall is ornamented with an inlaid wineglass. Each glass is stuffed with a red paper napkin—like a kerchief stuffed into the breast pocket of a suit coat. The floor is bedecked with sod.

'The relatively short duration of the event made it possible to use real sod,' says Ewoud. 'We moistened it every night using a plant sprayer. It held up surprisingly well.'

I try to imagine walking on the sod in high heels.

'It was our first aromatic design!' Ewoud exclaims.

'The sod helped absorb the noise,' says Edith. 'We thought the boxes would do the same thing, but the hardness of the material amplified the noise instead of reducing it.'

Sound insulation is a science. It's not surprising they got it wrong.

V.
ENGAGEMENT

We encounter situations in which Traast + Gruson set out to pique curiosity and arouse emotion. Impartiality is not an option.

Design comprises form and structure. While form attracts attention, structure brings a thing to life. Form establishes expectations; structure fulfills them. In the case of an exhibition, for instance, structure creates a sense of progress, moving the visitor toward a better appreciation and understanding of the subject matter. By virtue of the design, which is an explicit translation of the form and structure of the exhibition, visitors become engaged with the material in a way that resembles dialogue.

TRAAST + GRUSON's solution for an exhibition featuring commissioned photography in the Netherlands immediately engages the visitor's imagination because there is not, at first glance, a single photograph in sight.

The year is 1992. The venue: the impressive Commodities Hall of the Amsterdam Stock Exchange (often referred to as the Beurs van Berlage), a building designed by Dutch architect Hendrik Petrus Berlage (1856-1934). Berlage is considered the 'father of modern architecture' in the Netherlands.

The massive hall, measuring 1600 square meters, is dimly lit for the occasion. A collection of large, three-dimensional forms stands in the space. Twenty-seven small buildings of varying heights and widths create an impressive skyline. Doorways glow with yellow light emanating from the interiors. A small red darkroom light above each doorway signals 'enter,' as opposed to the customary 'keep out—photographer at work.'

TRAAST + GRUSON's design is a sort of visual pun. It presents the state (condition) of photography within the state (province) of photography (hence the architecture of the show). Each building houses a different commission. The interior settings say something about the work. For example, a project commissioned by a school district is presented in a classroom setting. A bistro-like environment houses the culinary commission. A solitary street lamp of the type typically found in Dutch villages stands in the space featuring architectural photographs commissioned by the village of Nagele. The street lamp was designed for Nagele in 1954 by Dutch architect designer Friso Kramer. The village itself was designed by Dutch architect Gerrit Rietveld, among others, including Aldo van Eijk, Mien Ruys, and Herman Hertzberger. According to TRAAST + GRUSON's design, one big show becomes twenty-seven small ones, each with its own message (form) and structure.

Dutch designer Jan van Toorn defines communication design as
visual journalism
with an emancipatory agenda.
The suggested emancipation has everything to do with how the communicated message is received; and this has everything to do with structure. Again, in the case of an exhibition, information is arranged in an effort to move visitors toward a specific conclusion or set of conclusions, which they use to form an opinion on the basis of their own backgrounds and experiences. Form makes certain instantaneous promises. For example: 'This exhibition is an entity.' Structure—intellectual, dramatic and emotional—upholds this central promise. Structural integrity ensures that the message is communicated accurately, clearly, and persuasively, captivating the visitor's imagination and enabling him to see the relevance and urgency of the new knowledge. A tall order, but one that design —as a discipline and as a response—nonetheless sets out to fulfill.

1994. Exhibition: Waar komt die naam vandaan? (Where does that name come from?). Venue: Kasteel Groeneveld, a magnificent 18th century country estate and park near the Dutch town of Baarn. Today the estate functions as an information center for the Ministry of Agriculture and Fisheries.

The exhibition sets out to answer the question posed by its title—thirteen times over. Thirteen place-names, some stemming from the ancient past and others with more contemporary roots, are selected with the intention of chronicling the origin and history of each, especially in relation to the landscape. TRAAST + GRUSON are responsible for the selection of names. They structure the exhibition and arrange the material to interest both the curious and the scholarly. Theirs is a chronological narrative as well as a subjective survey. The thirteen names appear within the context of a map of Holland re-created on the floor of the exhibition space. Certain names are accompanied by short descriptions that read like human-interest stories. This information prompts visitors to formulate their own responses to names referenced by the show. For instance, on seeing the name Nijmegen, a visitor may think, 'Aunt Truus was born there.' The visitor is motivated on a personal level, therefore, to learn more about where the name comes from.

Thirteen doors surround the space. Each door represents one of the names featured. Behind each door the history of one particular name is revealed. The material is extraordinarily complex. Names often represent an intermingling of historical fact and fantasy; the two are inseparable. TRAAST + GRUSON's solution simplifies the material without sacrificing the wealth of detail that makes it interesting and appealing to a diverse public. There is, quite literally, something for everyone. A combination of visual images, textual anecdotes, and relevant artifacts caters to the visitor's appetite for fact and thirst for fantasy. The design helps visitors not only to make sense of the material—and to make their way through it—but also to remember what they've learned. Illustrations reflect the style prevalent at the time the name originated, and artifacts reflect the period as well. These concrete visual elements are more easily remembered than abstract symbols, like words and numbers.

The exhibition has to be designed to travel. For this reason, TRAAST + GRUSON construct a space within a space. Prefab wood panels and doors combine to form the floor and walls of the exhibition. The elements fit together like puzzle pieces.

Overloon   Late middeleeuwen 1000-1500   Yzendijke   Nieuwe tijd 1500 -
Vlaardingen
Dorestate
Groningen   Hummelo   St. Oedenrode   Achttienhoven   Krabbendijke
Hengelo   Middelrode   Maartensdijk   Moerdijk
Bennebroek   Twaalfhoven   Munnikezijl
Eersel   Tienhoven   Nieuwersluis   Delfszijl   Eexterveen
Vreeswijk   Bommel   Velserbroek   Demmerik   Roelofarendsveen
Kockengen   's Heer Hendrikskinderen
Wijk en Aalburg
Medemblik   Munstergeleen
Gerkesklooster
Amsterdam
Wijk   Stavoren   Heerjansdam
bij   Kerkrade   Stellendam
Egmond   Kloosterrade
Duurstede   Buweklooster
Middelburg   's Heer Arendskerk
's Heer Abtskerke
Kootwijk   Heerhugowaard   Veendam
Ravenstein
Schoorl   Monnickendam
Meinerswijk   Ysselstein   Zuilen
Boskoop
Kesteren   Kester   Tasteren
Doornenburg
Rijn   Leeuwarden   Aardenburg   Ber
L   Nijmegen   Cuijk
Zeis   Maastricht   Cuijk
Utrecht
Wylre

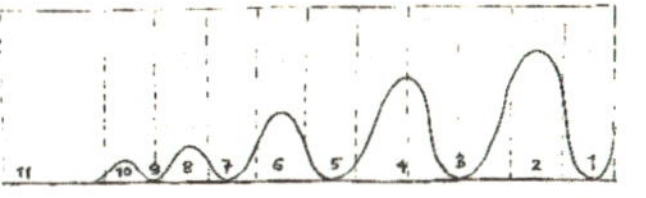

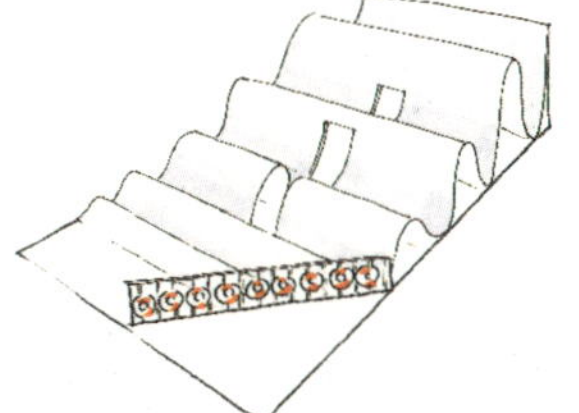

History is an attempt to recreate the past. It is a fitting together of various elements deemed appropriate, just, and relevant to the telling. What's included and what's left out depend on who's doing the narrating. H i s t o r y   i s   n e v e r   i m p a r t i a l . Context is significant as well. For instance, the history of the Titanic is inextricably bound up with popular culture, thanks in particular to Hollywood's latest cinematic rendition of the catastrophic event, told within the context of a fictional love story—as triumph in tragedy. The 1997 blockbuster is preceded by an American black-and-white film released in 1953, which also presents the story within the context of romantic destiny. Curiously, in 1943 the Germans made a film about the sinking of the British luxury liner as Nazi propaganda. And in 1915—three short years after the fatal event—a silent film featuring the Titanic was produced in Italy.

The year is 2000. The Prins Hendrik Maritime Museum in Rotterdam is hosting an exhibition entitled Ship of the Century. Selected by the public, the top ten ships represent the shipping industry in the twentieth century. Among them, of course, is the Titanic.

TRAAST + GRUSON create a series of cabin-like spaces in which to present the history unique to each ship. Context is provided by design. The curved roof lines of the cabins trace a wave-like motif in the space. The interior atmosphere of each cabin is distinctive. Not surprisingly, the space representing the Titanic spotlights the cinematic history of the ship—the Titanic as cultural icon.

ROTTERDAM
PORT SAID
CAIRO
SINGAPORE
CEYLON

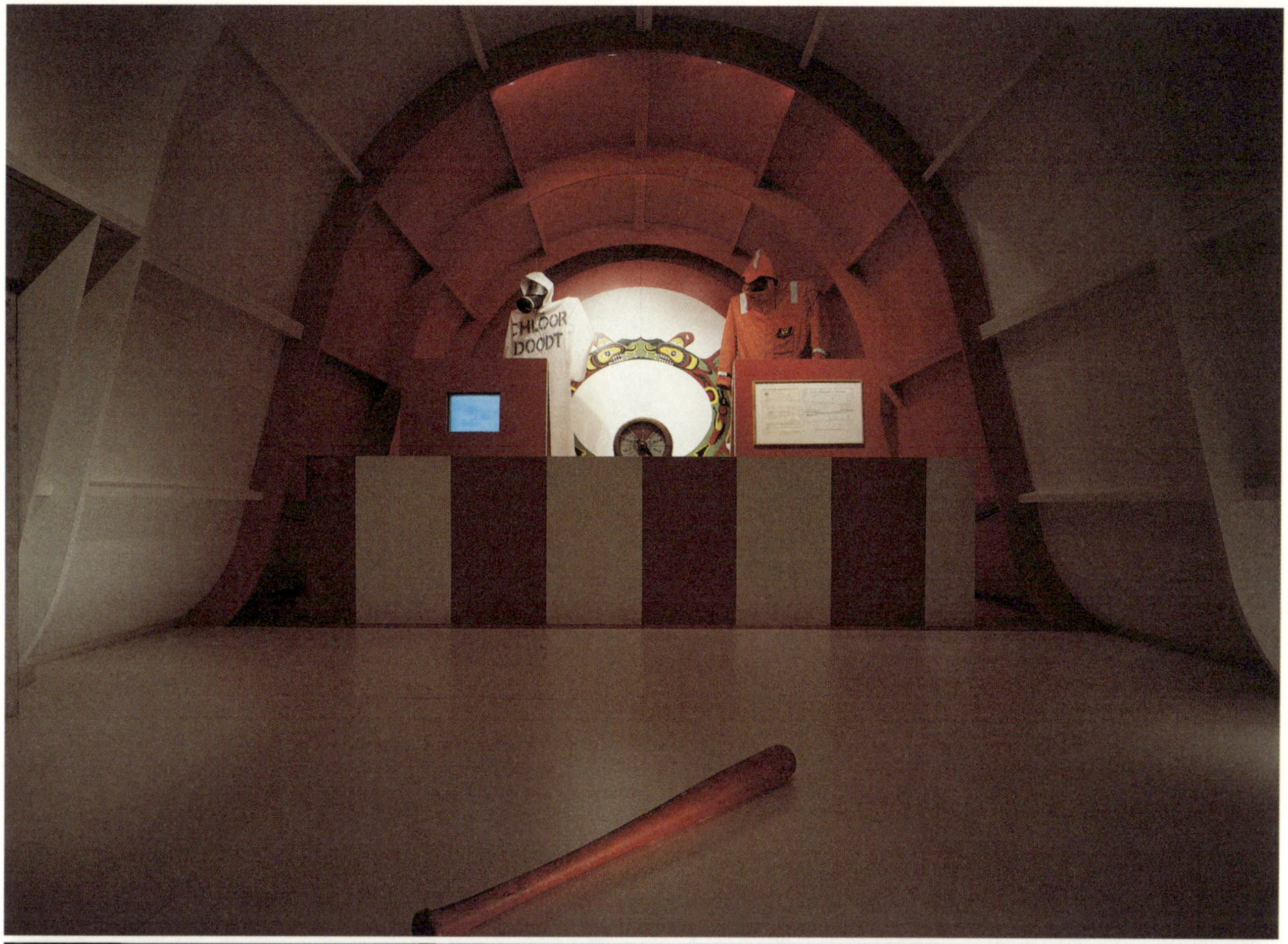

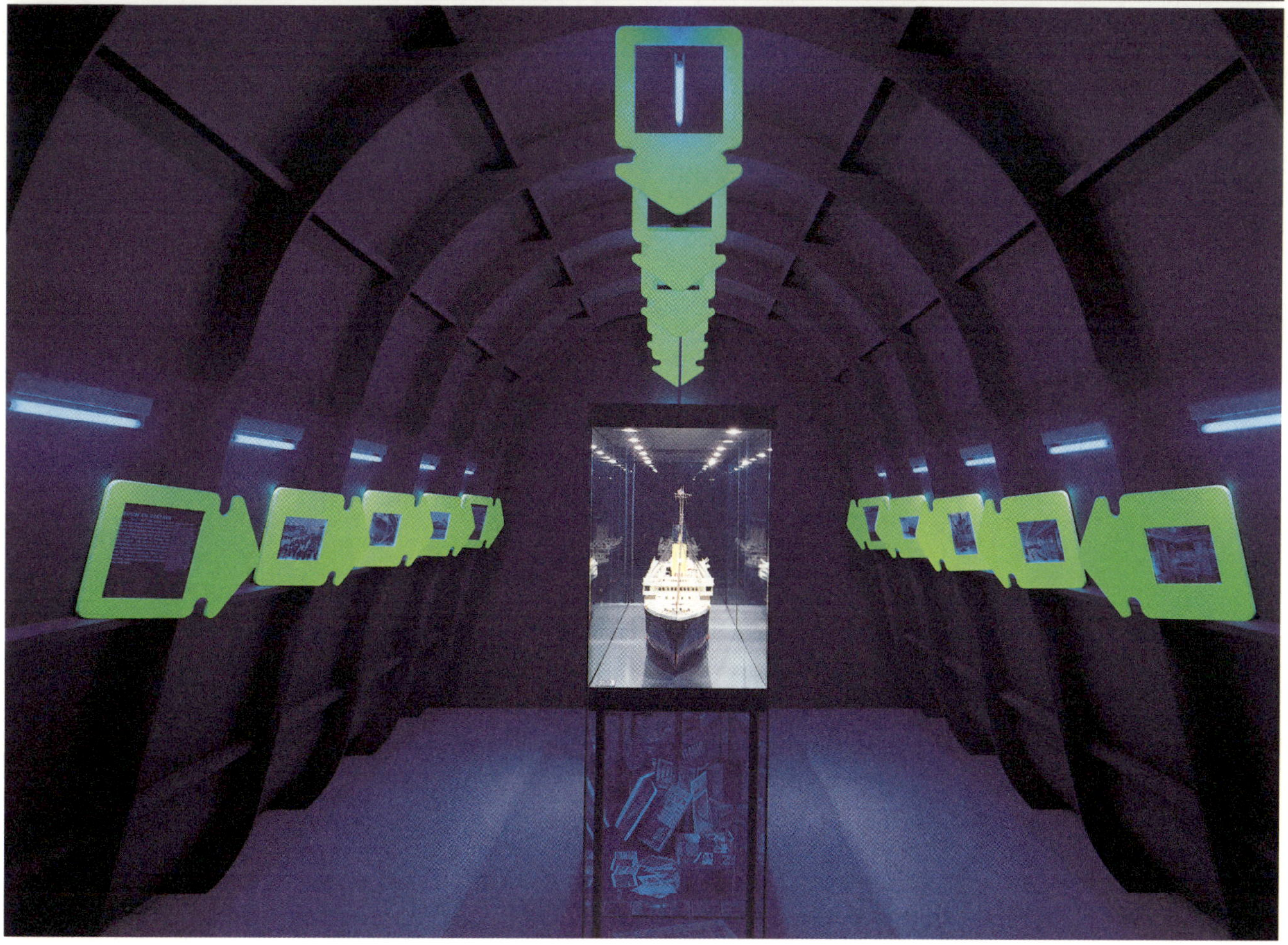

While TRAAST + GRUSON are free to interpret the historical material visually, one story they'd hoped to tell is rejected by organizers.

'Two ships in the show were built to sail between Indonesia and the Netherlands,' says Edith. 'Among the material for one of the ships we came across the diary of an Indonesian woman, written during her voyage to Holland. It's heart-wrenching stuff.'

'We wanted to tell the story of broken dreams,' Ewoud adds.

'She begins her diary with great enthusiasm for the coming voyage and expresses expectations of a better future,' Edith continues. 'But as the days pass into weeks, her mood shifts dramatically. Ultimately, her diary is testimony to the discrimination and abuse she endured at the hands of the Dutch.'

This wasn't the story the organizers wanted to tell. They advised TRAAST + GRUSON to focus on the hope the ship is believed to have inspired rather than the despair it proved to represent—for this woman and, no doubt, countless other Indonesian émigrés.
History?
Whose history?

DE LEEUW
AN UW KEUS
KAREL

F.W.F. Flexible Work Force | Olaf Stokb

Praktijk Berlin
school voor Kunsten, Arnhem
ekx | Hogeschool voor Kunsten, Arnhem
Bo 8

Smell?
What smell?
    Oh,

                         that.

        Upstairs.

            Just follow your nose.

The year is 1998. The venue: the Eindhoven Design Academy. The occasion: the results of a HEMA-sponsored design competition. Entrants are asked to design innovative, low-cost cleaning utensils. HEMA promises to produce and market the winning design.

    TRAAST + GRUSON use a cliché—clean as a whistle—as their point of departure.

    A house that looks clean
smells clean.

    In the past, the strong, sharp smell of ammonia screamed clean. When the less offensive pine and lemon scents were introduced in cleaning products, some consumers rejected them because they simply didn't smell clean enough. Today, people have an entirely different idea of what smells clean. Preferences vary among the whispering fragrances of

           lavender,

                 rose,

                    jasmine,

                        orange,

                            mint.

Liquid cleaning products, designed to smell good and look pretty, match the corresponding scents in an array of brilliant colors such as

                           magenta,

                    violet,

                yellow,

           tangerine,

      green.

TRAAST + GRUSON use these colorful liquid products to create a backdrop for the HEMA designs, of which there are thirty.

    Shallow plastic containers measuring 1 x 1 meter are arranged in two rows, back to back, on the concrete floor of the exhibition space: a long narrow hallway leading to the main entrance of the Design Academy. The containers are filled with liquid detergent. One is blue, one is pink, one is yellow, and so on. Poured out in such quantity, the liquid has a pearly quality to it, giving the color depth. The new designs are positioned just above the soapy surface. It's a vivid composition—not to mention a heady one!

    'No signage was necessary,' says Ewoud, grinning.

Exhibition design attempts to strike a balance between what is seen and what is said—
————between representation and presentation
————decoration and narration
————imitation and interpretation
integration and confrontation————.
So much depends on shared meaning.

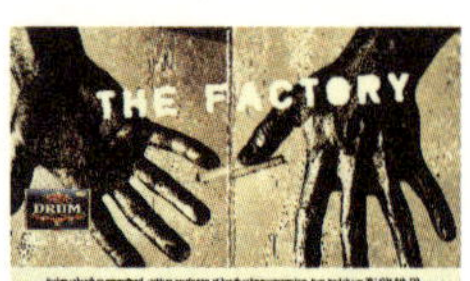

I'm reminded of a print advertising campaign that Koeweiden Postma created for Drum rolling tobacco. It comprises four simple elements, the first of which is a three-quarter-page, black-and-white photograph of two middle-aged hands, one palm up, the other palm down. The image also contains the words 'The Factory,' referencing the hands, and a small, full-color print of a pack of Drum tobacco above the word 'Self-made.' The white space beneath the photograph carries the mandatory warning about the dangers of smoking. The hands represent a consumer of Drum tobacco. My reading is much darker.
I see the tired hands of a low-wage tobacco fieldworker.

The year is 1990 and the city of Rotterdam, celebrating 650 years of existence, is looking ahead. Displayed in the main hall of the onetime passenger terminal of the Holland America Line are twenty-one proposed urban-renewal projects. Each is being considered by the municipal building authority as a possibility for development within the coming decade. The motivation for the exhibition is threefold: to present locations cited for redevelopment, to present architectural plans corresponding to each location, and to provide a platform for public discussion and debate on issues related to the proposed urban-renewal projects.

TRAAST + GRUSON divide the exhibition area into three equal sections. Taking the notion of development to heart, they have the first section represent a darkroom. Photographs of the targeted locations float in red fixer trays on wooden workstations—one photograph in each tray, several trays on each workstation. Red fluorescent strip lights illuminate the area. The second section mimics a warehouse. Made-to-measure wooden shipping crates, complete with packing straw and enameled identification tags, serve as pedestals and display cases for the maquettes, technical drawings, sketches, and other materials used to describe the various projects. White fluorescent light illuminates the area. Devoted to programming, the third section consists simply of a red lectern facing rows of chairs. The lectern is studded with stainless-steel standard-issue handles of the type used on shipping crates. The intention is purely decorative. (As I did when viewing the ad for Drum tobacco, I read something else into the design. In the present context, I connect the English word 'handle' with the Dutch word 'handel', meaning trade. With this link in mind, I see the handles as more than decoration. I associate them with the notion of trading ideas. To me, the lectern represents a point of negotiation and compromise.) The area is illuminated with multicolored fluorescent strip lights, which suggest a diversity of opinion that will no doubt characterize public programs organized to accompany the exhibition.

Het laboratorium
21 Stads-
vernieuwings-
projecten
UIT
7
8 9
6 5 4 3
1 2

3
4
8
2
1

Rotterdam revisited. The year is 1995 and thirty municipal and regional housing associations have joined forces. The umbrella organization is a commercial housing corporation called Maaskoepel. In an effort to formulate ideas about how the different associations can best cooperate with one other and, perhaps, even collaborate in the future, Maaskoepel has organized a three-day event entitled De Leefbaarheidsmarkt (The Quality of Life Fair).

TRAAST + GRUSON's design is extraordinarily simple. They create a campground with 'tents' designed to mimic the exaggerated styles of architecture that typify, for better or worse, many of Holland's new-build residential neighborhoods. Each association has its own tent, which it is responsible for furnishing according to its individual needs and agenda. The informal setting puts participants at ease and, as happens on camping trips, creates a sense of belonging.

'One group of serious campers,' says Edith, smiling, 'brought their own food and refreshments. They even brought a refrigerator.'

'People behave differently at a campground,' says Ewoud. 'They make more of an effort to get to know each other. I've come home from camping trips knowing more about my neighbors there than I do about my neighbors here at home!'

I, on the other hand, am not partial to camping, so the idea of spending three days at a mock campground leaves me cold.

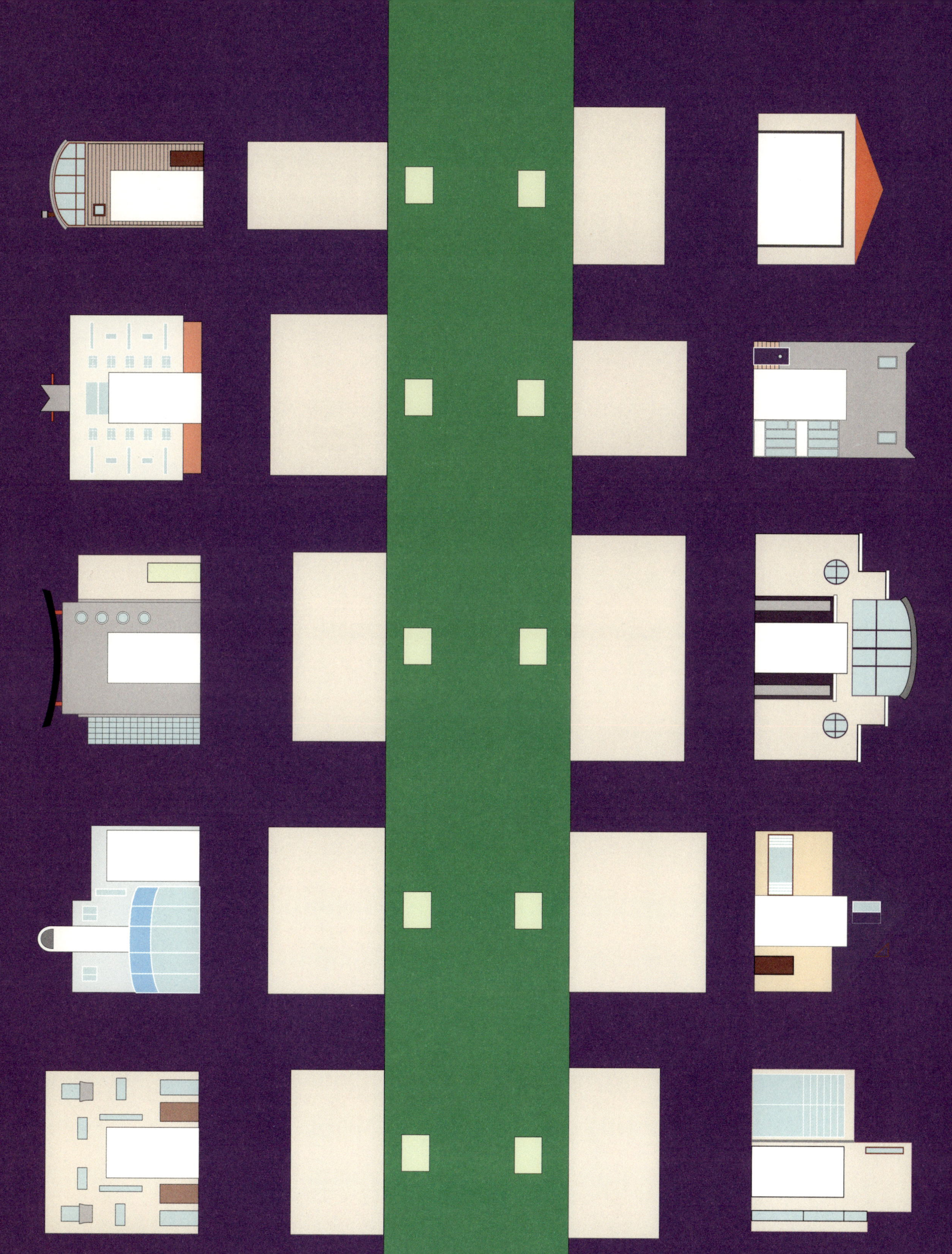

Markets, like people, are fickle. So are manufacturers. 'We love your idea!' exclaims a furniture manufacturer, responding to a young designer's seating concept on display at an international fair. Later, when the designer follows up, the manufacturer hesitates before adding, with far less enthusiasm, 'Your design will have to be modified.' In other words, the original design is too costly to produce, so modifications are needed (read: revamp the concept) to make it profitable. It's a common occurrence and one that furniture designers have had to learn to live with. Until now.

Hidden is the name of a Dutch manufacturer whose mandate is to produce new furniture designs in the same unadulterated form in which they are conceived. No giving in, nothing hidden. On the contrary. The manufacturer is committed to locating the appropriate technologies, and to engaging the skill and expertise of the people behind these technologies, in an effort to turn ideas into reality.

In his epic novel, *Les Misérables* (1862),
Victor Hugo wrote
Where the telescope ends, the microscope begins.
Which of the two has a grander view?

Indeed. Both instruments give us the possibility to see the invisible—to discover that which would otherwise remain hidden from the naked eye. This is TRAAST + GRUSON's point of departure for their design of the first Hidden show.

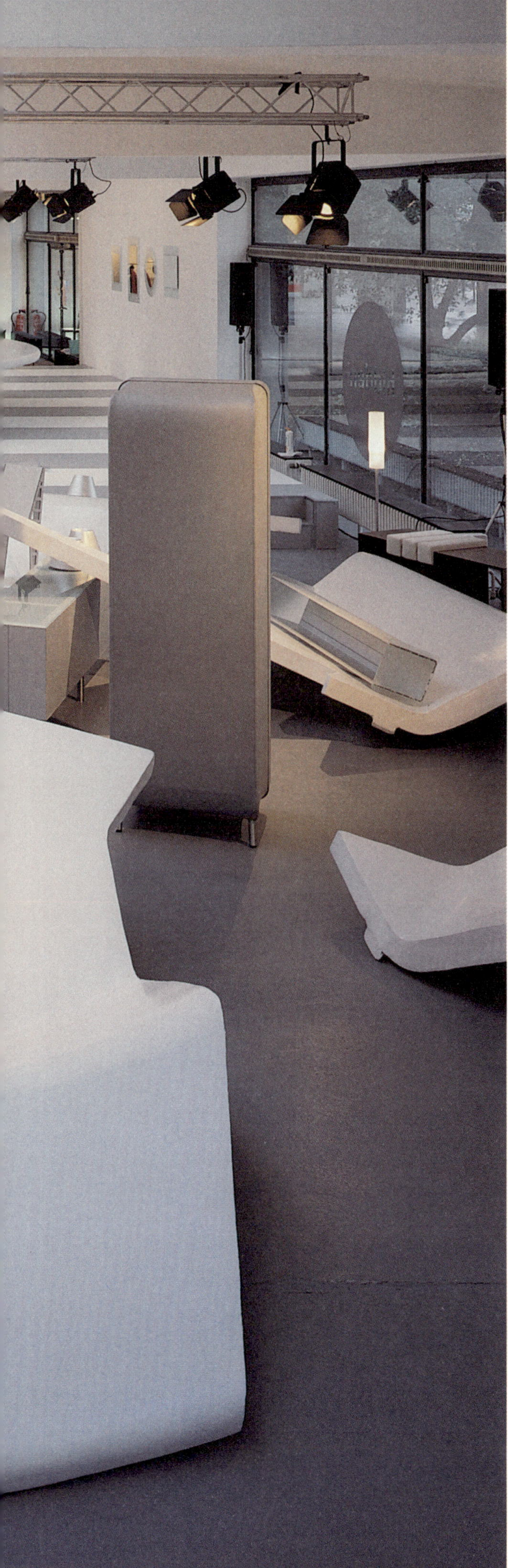

The year is 1999. A Dutch enterprise, Hidden, is celebrating its introduction at the International Furniture Fair in Cologne, Germany. The company has an area of 100 square meters at the fair and an additional 400 at the Kölnische Kunstverein, a local art gallery. The reason for the two locations is simple: the objects at the fair are furniture, but a gallery setting makes them art.

TRAAST + GRUSON's design for the furniture fair is straightforward and not at all that interesting—a stark contrast to the presentation designed for the gallery, which depicts an enormous place setting: plate, glass, cutlery. The plate functions as a bar at which visitors can gather, and it doubles as a stage. Furniture designs pose in the center of the giant form like petits fours on a plate. Visitors can look but not touch; the furniture is safely out of reach. A second plate is shattered. Its contents—another selection of furniture designs—are scattered about but remain upright. This part of the show is hands-on. Visitors are encouraged to touch the furniture, to lean on it, sit on it, open it, experience it.

117

2000. A new collection of Hidden designs is on display at the International Furniture Fair in Milan and at the Spazio Consolo Milano, an art gallery. The company has 45 square meters of space at the fair and 300 at the gallery.

TRAAST + GRUSON maintain the concept they developed for the 1999 Hidden exposition in Cologne. This time the design depicts a giant bedroom scene. At the fair, a huge keyhole provides visitors with a glimpse of Hidden designs displayed in a tidy bedroom. Each piece is carefully illuminated for maximum visibility.

In contrast to the display at the fair, the gallery presentation features a disorderly, though still king-size, scene. The bedroom is messy. Gigantic articles of clothing have been carelessly discarded—a bra, high heels, stockings. Hidden designs are part of the chaos. Stepping through another huge keyhole, visitors become part of what for some is a familiar scene.

TRAAST + GRUSON's collaboration with Hidden ends after the second year, when Hidden decides to involve its own designers in the creation of future shows.

'*Designing an exhibit is different from designing a chair,*' says Edith, questioning the expediency of asking a furniture designer to design a show.

Designers working for designers
—it's a tricky, sometimes sticky business.

All
good
things
come
to
an
end.

Projects are initiated, created, and produced. Other projects follow. I experience such endings with mixed feelings. A sense of accomplishment is always met with thoughts of how things could have been handled differently. In retrospect, the mind is invariably flooded with a slew of fresh ideas and insights. This can be discouraging, but it needn't be. Such things are better carried over into the next project, as lessons learned.

The thing I will never get used to is the transient relationships that characterize most projects. For me, getting inside a subject means personalizing it, developing a closeness to the individuals who help bring it to life. In this case, Edith and Ewoud. Their work was new to me when I took on this project. Getting to know them and their work inspired and shaped the ideas presented in this book.

Edith and Ewoud.

Idealists.

Iconoclasts.

I bid you adieu.

Photography
Ewoud Traast

▶ Page 7
▶ Project title HEMA backpacks
▶ Client HEMA, *HEMA, a Dutch department store*
▶ Subject Design competition featuring fifty-five backpack designs
▶ Year 1999
▶ Venue Het Museon, *Het Museon Science Museum, The Hague, the Netherlands*
▶ Duration One month
▶ Budget EUR 12,000
▶ Floor space 400m^2
▶ Estimated number of visitors A few hundred
▶ Most memorable aspect for the designers We had an urge to assault either the contact person or the client, or both, with one of the backpacks.

Photography
Ernst Moritz

▶ Page 10
▶ Project title De Frans Hals Prijs 1992 voor tentoonstelling-ontwerpen rondom Het Droste Effect, *The Frans Hals Prize 1992 for exhibition designs featuring Het Droste Effect, or 'the Illusion of Infinity'*
▶ Client Frans Hals Museum
▶ Subject The art of exhibition design: four teams are invited to design an exhibition featuring the visual phenomenon known as Het Droste Effect, or 'the Illusion of Infinity'
▶ Year 1992
▶ Venue De Vishal, *The Fish Hall, Frans Hals Museum, Haarlem, the Netherlands*
▶ Duration The four exhibition concepts were briefly displayed, but none was ever realized.
▶ Budget EUR 880 (design fee)
▶ Floor space 60m^2
▶ Most memorable aspect for the designers We consider this one of our more important exhibition designs because of its conceptual strength. It not only represents a reaction to the subject, as interpretation, but also contributes to the thinking that informs the subject, as explanation. What interested us most, and what we were motivated to discover for ourselves, is how Het Droste Effect relates to life—the life cycles of Nature and the cycle of life in general. In our opinion, the design is a clear demonstration of our capacity to generate new ideas and to influence editorial content in a profound and compelling way.

122

Photography
Ernst Moritz

▶ Page 12
▶ Project title Integraal Project Noordrand, *Integral Project for the North Rim*
▶ Client Gemeente Rotterdam, Stadsontwikkeling, *Municipality of Rotterdam, Department of Urban Development*
▶ Subject Plans for the redevelopment of Rotterdam's Noordrand area. The central question: to move or not to move Zestienhoven, the municipal airport
▶ Year 1991
▶ Venue De Doelen Muziek Theater, *De Doelen Music Theater, Rotterdam, the Netherlands*
▶ Duration One day, after which the show traveled to different locations throughout the country
▶ Budget EUR 22,000

- ▶ Floor space 80m²
- ▶ Estimated number of visitors 150
- ▶ Most memorable aspect for the designers A bit of unplanned humor: In a country defined by water—a nation in which so much land has been reclaimed from the sea—we had to laugh when we touched the knobs on the puzzle pieces representing water and discovered they were loose.

Photography
Ernst Moritz

- ▶ Page 14
- ▶ Project title Restauratie grafmonument Willem van Oranje, *Restoration of the Monument to William of Orange*
- ▶ Client Rijksgebouwendienst, *Government Building Agency*
- ▶ Subject An exhibition designed to enable the public to follow the progress of a five-year restoration project
- ▶ Year 1995
- ▶ Venue Nieuwe Kerk, *New Church, Delft, the Netherlands*
- ▶ Duration Five years
- ▶ Budget EUR 75,000
- ▶ Floor space 600m²
- ▶ Estimated number of visitors 100,000 a year
- ▶ Most memorable aspect for the designers The 'responsive' nature of the stained glass representation of the monument worked extremely well.

Photography
Ewoud Traast

- ▶ Page 22
- ▶ Project title Rotterdam Danst, *Rotterdam Dances*
- ▶ Client Rotterdamse Kunst Stichting, *Rotterdam Art Foundation*
- ▶ Subject Classical dance festival and competition
- ▶ Year 1990
- ▶ Venue De Doelen Muziek Theater, *De Doelen Music Theater, Rotterdam, the Netherlands*
- ▶ Duration One weekend
- ▶ Budget EUR 6,800
- ▶ Floor space Foyer measuring 200 x 4 meters
- ▶ Estimated number of visitors A few hundred
- ▶ Most memorable aspect for the designers A crowd gathered on one of the red heart-shaped carpets appeared reluctant to set as much as a single chair leg or one foot outside the boundary of the carpet—they treated the surrounding linoleum as if it were water (reminiscent of the games children play).

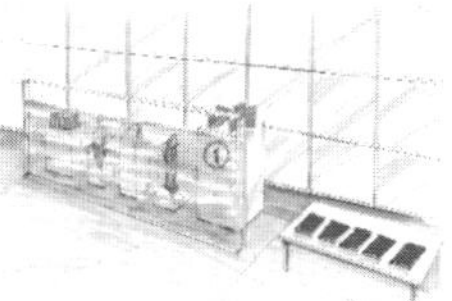

Drawing
Alicia Blokland

- ▶ Page 23
- ▶ Project title Het Maasbeeld, *Maas River Sculpture*
- ▶ Client Rotterdamse Kunst Stichting, *Rotterdam Art Foundation*
- ▶ Subject Presentation of the winning design and four runners-up for a sculpture with a Maas River theme
- ▶ Year 1990
- ▶ Venue Hal, Holland-Amerika Lijn Hall, *Holland America Line, Rotterdam, the Netherlands*
- ▶ Duration Four weeks
- ▶ Budget EUR 11,500
- ▶ Floor space 10m²
- ▶ Estimated number of visitors A few thousand (the presentation was part of a larger exhibition hosted by the Rotterdam Department of Public Works)
- ▶ Most memorable aspect for the designers A day before the opening, the custom-built aquarium, which formed the focal point of

the show, burst, flooding the floor. The aquarium was too tall, too long, and too narrow to withstand the immense pressure of the water it was designed to contain.

▶ <u>Page</u> 18
▶ <u>Project title</u> Boundaries of the Postage Stamp
▶ <u>Client</u> Afdeling Kunst en Vormgeving van de voormalig PTT, *Department of Art and Design of the former PTT*
▶ <u>Subject</u> Exhibition of twelve new-issue postage stamps created by graphic designers representing the twelve countries of the European Union, and a forum focusing on the reputation and quality of graphic design in these various countries
▶ <u>Year</u> 1993
▶ <u>Venue</u> Jan van Eyck Akademie, *Jan van Eyck Academy, Maastricht, the Netherlands*
▶ <u>Duration</u> Exhibition: three weeks; forum: three days
▶ <u>Budget</u> EUR 15,900
▶ <u>Floor space</u> 120m²
▶ <u>Estimated number of visitors</u> Exhibition: 50 a day; forum: 300
▶ <u>Most memorable aspect for the designers</u> The Dutch designer invited to exhibit his work didn't respond to our repeated appeals for materials—sketches, technical drawings, and the like—until we told him that the size of the table built to display his design depended entirely on the amount of material he submitted. Soon after, we received piles of stuff from him.

▶ <u>Page</u> 24
▶ <u>Project title</u> Play House
▶ <u>Client</u> Droog Design for Bang & Olufsen
▶ <u>Subject</u> Presentation of the latest Bang & Olufsen audiovisual equipment
▶ <u>Year</u> 1999
▶ <u>Venue</u> Salone Internazionale del Mobile, *International Furniture Fair, Milan, Italy*
▶ <u>Duration</u> One week
▶ <u>Budget</u> EUR 28,200
▶ <u>Floor space</u> 500m²
▶ <u>Estimated number of visitors</u> A few hundred a day
▶ <u>Most memorable aspect for the designers</u> Despite the open structure of the design, visitors chose to enter the imaginary apartment through the front door.

▶ <u>Page</u> 29
▶ <u>Project title</u> Forumdiscussie Beeldende Kunst Nota Forum *Discussion on New Legislation for Public Support of the Arts*
▶ <u>Client</u> Rotterdamse Kunststichting Rotterdam Art Foundation
▶ <u>Subject</u> Forum for discussing the pros and cons of new legislation regarding public support for visual artists
▶ <u>Year</u> 1987
▶ <u>Venue</u> Zaal de Unie, *The Union, Rotterdam, the Netherlands*
▶ <u>Duration</u> One evening
▶ <u>Budget</u> EUR 8,200
▶ <u>Floor space</u> 70m²
▶ <u>Estimated number of visitors</u> 100
▶ <u>Most memorable aspect for the designers</u> Whether or not panelists actively participated in the discussions, their moods were clearly registered by the tall chair backs designed as part of the décor. The more agitated a panelist became, the more his chair

back vibrated. We also noticed that one of the panelists was wearing a sweater the same color as his chair—a coincidence?

Photography
Ernst Moritz

▶ Page 31
▶ Project title Rotterdam Film Festival Restaurant
▶ Client Le Muniche Restaurant
▶ Subject Temporary interior design for Le Muniche, a restaurant in Rotterdam's Hotel Central that served vegetarian meals for the duration of the film festival
▶ Year 1991
▶ Venue Hotel Central, Rotterdam, the Netherlands
▶ Duration One week
▶ Budget EUR 3,400
▶ Floor space 100m²
▶ Estimated number of visitors 100 an evening
▶ Most memorable aspect for the designers Arriving in the parking lot of a huge abbatoir, we were startled by the sight of a bloody pig's foot lying on the tarmac.

Photography
Ernst Moritz

▶ Page 33
▶ Project title Wakker worden, *Wake up!*
▶ Client HEMA, *HEMA, a Dutch department store*
▶ Subject Design competition featuring fifty new alarm-clock designs
▶ Year 1996
▶ Venue Centraal Museum, Utrecht, the Netherlands
▶ Duration One month
▶ Budget EUR 4,500
▶ Floor space 250m²
▶ Estimated number of visitors A few hundred
▶ Most memorable aspect for the designers We sold the rooster stands after the exhibition. One of the buyers was a poultyman named Mr. De Haan (de haan is Dutch for 'the rooster').

Photography
Mischa Keijser

▶ Page 38
▶ Project title Afscheid Bram Peper, *Farewell Bram Peper*
▶ Client City of Rotterdam
▶ Subject Design of an event organized as a farewell party for Rotterdam's former mayor, Bram Peper
▶ Year 1998
▶ Venue De Doelen Muziek Theater, *De Doelen Music Theater, Rotterdam, the Netherlands*
▶ Duration One day
▶ Budget EUR 20,400
▶ Floor space 600m²
▶ Estimated number of visitors 1500
▶ Most memorable aspect for the designers In contrast to most assignments, we arrived at the design solution for this event in about five minutes.

Photography
Ernst Moritz

▶ Page 40
▶ Project title At Home in the City
▶ Client Europan 3, Nederlands Architectuur Instituut, *Europan 3 Netherlands Architecture Institute*
▶ Subject An exposition of forty-four award-winning projects and forty-one honorable mentions developed for fifty-two selected European cities and conceived within the context of the theme 'At Home in the City'

▶ Year 1994
▶ Venue Nederlands Archtectuur Instituut Netherlands,
Architecture Institute, Rotterdam, the Netherlands
▶ Duration Five weeks
▶ Budget EUR 114,000
▶ Floor space 600m²
▶ Estimated number of visitors A few thousand
▶ Most memorable aspect for the designers Visitors actually used
the shopping carts, politely returning them to their proper place
after viewing the exhibition. They also threw their trash into
the garbage cans, which were used, like the shopping carts, to
create physical borders in the space.

Photography
Ernst Moritz

▶ Page 44
▶ Project title De voelbare leegte, *The Tangible Emptiness*
▶ Client Het Museon
▶ Subject An exhibition based on the ritual of death as it has been
interpreted and experienced by the Dutch for the past 2000
years
▶ Year 1999
▶ Venue Het Museon, *Het Museon Science Museum, The Hague,
the Netherlands*
▶ Duration Five months
▶ Budget EUR 80,000
▶ Floor space 200m²
▶ Estimated number of visitors A few thousand
▶ Most memorable aspect for the designers The evening before the
opening, the historian responsible for the exhibition was still
huddled over his laptop, looking pretty close to death himself.

Photography
Ernst Moritz

▶ Page 50
▶ Project title Rotterdam 2045
▶ Client Manifestatie 50 jaar Wederopbouw, Gemeente Rotterdam,
*Organization Celebrating 50 years of Postwar Reconstruction,
Municipality of Rotterdam*
▶ Subject Five evenings of public debate on the subject of urban
planning and development in the coming five decades, focusing
on economic, social, structural, environmental, and political
issues
▶ Year 1995
▶ Venue Laurens Kerk, *St. Laurens Church, Rotterdam,
the Netherlands*
▶ Duration Five evenings
▶ Budget EUR 11,300
▶ Floor space 5000m² plus 25 m²
▶ Estimated number of visitors A few hundred every evening
▶ Most memorable aspect for the designers Working in the church
we felt, once again, 'at home in the city.'

Photography
Ernst Moritz

▶ Page 54
▶ Project title Het Mega-Effect, *The Mega-Effect*
▶ Client ECT, Europe Combined Terminals
▶ Subject An exposition celebrating twenty-five years of ECT, one
of the world's largest container transshipment companies
▶ Year 1992
▶ Venue Cleaning center ('car wash') for containers, Port of Rotterdam,
the Netherlands
▶ Duration One week

▶ Budget EUR 82,000
▶ Floor space 1500m²
▶ Estimated number of visitors A few thousand
▶ Most memorable aspect for the designers The political aim of the exposition was the promotion of the Betuwe railroad line, but there was no mention of this in the brief, which stated that the event was in honor of the company's twenty-five-year history. Had we been aware of the political underpinnings, we would have placed more emphasis on the human side of the story.

Photography
Ernst Moritz

▶ Page 59
▶ Project title Die 100 schönsten Bücher aus den Niederlanden und Flandern, *The 100 Best Book Designs from the Netherlands and Flanders*
▶ Client CPNB, de Rijksdienst Beeldende Kunst CPNB, *Collective Propaganda for Dutch Books and the National Agency of the Arts*
▶ Subject The one hundred most beautifully designed books published in the Netherlands and the Dutch-speaking part of Belgium over the past six years
▶ Year 1993
▶ Venue Frankfurter Buchmesse, *Frankfurt Book Fair, Frankfurt, Germany*
▶ Duration Five days
▶ Budget EUR 20,500
▶ Floor space 80m²
▶ Estimated number of visitors Several hundred a day
▶ Most memorable aspect for the designers We had fun selecting a variety of tacky logos from the Yellow Pages, all of which were chosen for their explicit, albeit crass, visual qualities.

Photography
Ewoud Traast

▶ Page 61
▶ Project title VideoRom, Biennale de Valencia, *VideoRom, Valencia Biennial*
▶ Client Droog Design
▶ Subject A mobile video theater for presenting a selection of art videos at regular intervals during the biennial at various preselected locations in Valencia
▶ Year 2001
▶ Duration Five months
▶ Budget EUR 27,000
▶ Floor space Vehicle and projection unit: from 25m² to 130m²
▶ Estimated number of visitors A few hundred a day
▶ Most memorable aspect for the designers When we delivered the mobile projection unit (we'd rented the vehicle from a Dutch company, applied the design, and driven the truck to Valencia), we were surprised to find no one in charge. Nothing in the way of permissions had been organized for the official opening of the Biennial. Talk about discouraging! And don't forget to mention that never in our fourteen years as a design team have we eaten such salty food.

Photography
Ernst Moritz

▶ Page 64
▶ Project title De Stijlkamers, *The Theme Rooms*
▶ Client Centraal Museum, Utrecht, the Netherlands
▶ Subject A series of theme rooms highlighting different aspects of
▶ the museum's collections
▶ Year 2000

- ► <u>Venue</u> Centraal Museum, Utrecht, the Netherlands
- ► <u>Duration</u> Four months
- ► <u>Budget</u> EUR 11,000
- ► <u>Floor space</u> Each room: 20m²
- ► <u>Estimated number of visitors</u> A few hundred
- ► <u>Most memorable aspect for the designers</u> In the room featuring seventeenth-century cityscapes, the blue paint applied to walls, floor and ceiling perfectly complemented the warm tones used in the paintings. The canvases appeared luminous in the totally blue space.

Photography
Ernst Moritz

- ► <u>Page</u> 70
- ► <u>Project title</u> Signs of the street
- ► <u>Client</u> Rijksdienst Beeldende Kunst, *National Agency of the Arts*
- ► <u>Subject</u> An exposition of PTT-initiated design throughout the decennia
- ► <u>Year</u> 1992
- ► <u>Venue</u> Triennale di Milano, Milan, Italy
- ► <u>Duration</u> Three months
- ► <u>Budget</u> 37,000
- ► <u>Floor space</u> 350m²
- ► <u>Estimated number of visitors</u> A few thousand
- ► <u>Most memorable aspect for the designers</u> Everything was prefab. The only thing we didn't have was sandbags to anchor the flats. To our consternation it took us a week to find a place in Milan that sold sandbags.

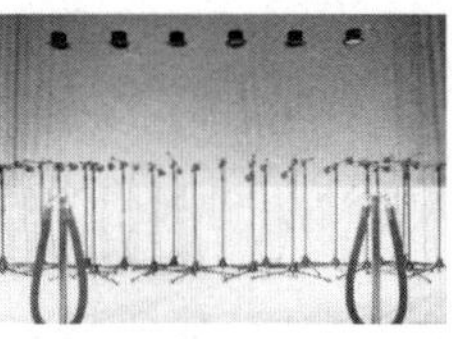

Photography
Ewoud Traast

- ► <u>Page</u> 75
- ► <u>Project title</u> Nationaal Theaterfestival, *National Theater Festival*
- ► <u>Client</u> Het National Theaterfestival, *National Theater Festival*
- ► <u>Subject</u> Décor design for the lobby of the Rotterdam Playhouse, including a platform for panel discussions
- ► <u>Year</u> 1989
- ► <u>Venue</u> Schouwburg Playhouse, Rotterdam, the Netherlands
- ► <u>Duration</u> One week
- ► <u>Budget</u> EUR 11,300
- ► <u>Floor space</u> Lobby: 400m²; platform: 30m²
- ► <u>Estimated number of visitors</u> A few hundred a day
- ► <u>Most memorable aspect for the designers</u> Actors who are used to playing different roles and to wearing costumes refused to discuss theater-related issues from a platform that positioned top hats above their heads and red clown-like microphone covers in front of their noses.

Photography
Ernst Moritz

- ► <u>Page</u> 77
- ► <u>Project title</u> Who's Afraid of Ancient Blue?
- ► <u>Client</u> Rijksmuseum van Oudheden, *National Museum of Antiquities*
- ► <u>Subject</u> A temporary installation of Egyptian sarcophagi and Roman busts on view during museum renovations lasting two years
- ► <u>Year</u> 1997
- ► <u>Venue</u> Rijksmuseum van Oudheden, *National Museum of Antiquities, Leiden, the Netherlands*
- ► <u>Duration</u> Two years
- ► <u>Budget</u> EUR 45,500
- ► <u>Floor space</u> 1000m²
- ► <u>Estimated number of visitors</u> A few thousand

▶ Most memorable aspect The huge blue tarpaulin suspended from the ceiling of the Taffeh gallery, which represented the sky, was used later to cover windows in an upstairs gallery featuring an exhibition on the Mediterranean, this time representing the sea. Two for the price of one.

Photography
Mischa Keijser

▶ Page 80
▶ Project title Oranienbaum
▶ Client Droog Design
▶ Subject An exhibition of products created by Droog Design for the Oranienbaum Estate in Germany, and glassware for Salviati
▶ Year 1999
▶ Venue Salone Internazionale del Mobile, *International Furniture Fair, Milan, Italy*
▶ Duration One week
▶ Budget EUR 27,000
▶ Floor space 400m²
▶ Estimated number of visitors A few hundred a day
▶ Most memorable aspect for the designers The fountain was built to display the glassware for Salviati, but we had no idea what the objects themselves looked like. To our surprise, the glass-ware designs closely resembled the water droplets generated by the bubbling fountain.

Photography
Ernst Moritz

▶ Page 84
▶ Project title 1000 jaar markten in de Domstad, *1000 Years of Markets in Cathedral City*
▶ Client Centraal Museum, Utrecht, the Netherlands
▶ Subject The history of Utrecht, from its origin as a small trading town to the present day
▶ Year 2001
▶ Venue Centraal Museum, Utrecht, the Netherlands
▶ Duration Five months
▶ Budget EUR 22,700, plus the assistance of in-house builders and technicians
▶ Floor space 700m²
▶ Estimated number of visitors A few hundred
▶ Most memorable aspect for the designers We were given a private tour of the museum's extensive depot, including a privileged look at art objects and paintings not connected with the show we were hired to design.

Photography
Ernst Moritz

▶ Page 86
▶ Project title Kwaliteit van het wonen in de jaren '90, *Housing Quality in the Nineties*
▶ Client Werkgroep 5x5 *Study Group 5x5*
▶ Subject Five-day event focusing on innovative solutions to urban planning and residential development in the 1990s in the Netherlands
▶ Year 1989
▶ Venue Hal, Holland Amerika Lijn Hall, *Holland America Line, Rotterdam, the Netherlands*
▶ Duration Five days
▶ Budget EUR 15,900
▶ Floor space 2,800m²
▶ Estimated number of visitors A few hundred a day
▶ Most memorable aspect for the designers We believe great

effects can be achieved with the simplest of means. This event proved how true that can be. Even we were surprised by the monumental effect created by the multiplication of simple run-of-the-mill materials.

Photography
Ernst Moritz

▶ Page 92
▶ Project title Fotowerk, *Photo Work*
▶ Client Stichting Perspectief, *Perspective Foundation*
▶ Subject Commissioned photography in the Netherlands
▶ Year 1992
▶ Venue Beurs van Berlage, *Amsterdam Stock Exchange, Amsterdam, the Netherlands*
▶ Duration Three weeks
▶ Budget EUR 38,600
▶ Floor space 1200m²
▶ Estimated number of visitors Thousands
▶ Most memorable aspect for the designers We designed, constructed, transported, and built the show in a matter of days for a very low budget. (Thanks, again, to our friends for all their help.)

Photography
Ernst Moritz

▶ Page 98
▶ Project title Waar komt die naam vandaan? *Where Does that Name Come From?*
▶ Client Kasteel Groeneveld, Ministerie van Landbouw en Visserij, *Castle Groeneveld and the Ministry of Agriculture and Fisheries*
▶ Subject An exhibition featuring the origin of place names from the ancient past to the present day, especially in relation to the landscape
▶ Year 1994
▶ Venue Kasteel Groeneveld, *Castle Groeneveld, Baarn, the Netherlands*
▶ Duration Three months
▶ Budget EUR 38,000
▶ Floor space 100m²
▶ Estimated number of visitors Several thousand
▶ Most memorable aspect for the designers The irreconcilable and untemperable battle among historians regarding the true origin of place names rages on!

Photography
Ernst Moritz

▶ Page 101
▶ Project title Het Schip van de Eeuw, *Ship of the Century*
▶ Client Het Maritiem Museum Prins Hendrik, *Prince Hendrik Maritime Museum*
▶ Subject An exhibition featuring the top ten ships, selected by the public, representative of the shipping industry in the twentieth century
▶ Year 2000
▶ Venue Maritiem Museum Prins Hendrik, *Prince Hendrik Maritime Museum, Rotterdam, the Netherlands*
▶ Duration Eight months
▶ Budget EUR 36,400, plus the assistance of in-house builders and technicians
▶ Floor space 500m²
▶ Estimated number of visitors A few thousand
▶ Most memorable aspect for the designers During the presentation of the design concept, the client asked: What do the waves signify?

Photography
Ewoud Traast

▶ <u>Page</u> 108
▶ <u>Project title</u> Schoonmaken, *Clean Up*
▶ <u>Client</u> HEMA, *HEMA, a Dutch department store*
▶ <u>Subject</u> An exposition featuring the results of a HEMA-sponsored design competition for innovative, low-cost cleaning utensils
▶ <u>Year</u> 1998
▶ <u>Venue</u> De Witte Dame, Eindhoven, the Netherlands
▶ <u>Duration</u> One month
▶ <u>Budget</u> EUR 6,800
▶ <u>Floor space</u> 30m²
▶ <u>Estimated number of visitors</u> A few hundred
▶ <u>Most memorable aspect for the designers</u> No routing system was needed. Visitors simply followed their noses.

Photography
Ernst Moritz

▶ <u>Page</u> 110
▶ <u>Project title</u> Het laboratorium, *The Laboratory*
▶ <u>Client</u> 650 jaar Rotterdam, *Rotterdam 650 Years*
▶ <u>Subject</u> Presentation of twenty-one proposed urban-renewal projects for the city of Rotterdam
▶ <u>Year</u> 1990
▶ <u>Venue</u> Hal, Holland Amerika Lijn Hall, *Holland America Line, Rotterdam, the Netherlands*
▶ <u>Duration</u> Three months
▶ <u>Budget</u> EUR 40,000
▶ <u>Floor space</u> 1,000m²
▶ <u>Estimated number of visitors</u> A few thousand
▶ <u>Most memorable aspect for the designers</u> No one disturbed the plasticized photographs submerged in trays of water in the mock-darkroom, assuming (perhaps) that the liquid was a chemical fixer.

131

Photography
Stijn Brakkee

▶ <u>Page</u> 112
▶ <u>Project title</u> De leefbaarheidsmarkt, *The Quality of Life Fair*
▶ <u>Client</u> De Maaskoepel
▶ <u>Subject</u> A three-day event during which thirty municipal and regional housing associations shared ideas and experiences with an eye to future collaboration
▶ <u>Year</u> 1995
▶ <u>Venue</u> Hal 4, *Hall 4, Rotterdam, the Netherlands*
▶ <u>Duration</u> Three days
▶ <u>Budget</u> EUR 31,000
▶ <u>Floor space</u> 600m²
▶ <u>Estimated number of visitors</u> A few hundred
▶ <u>Most memorable aspect for the designers</u> We had fun researching the different postmodern, and often outlandish, architectural styles in the Rotterdam region, such as pseudo-Islamic and pseudo-farm style (we called it party-hat architecture), examples of which we used for our design.

Photography
Ernst Moritz

▶ <u>Page</u> 114
▶ <u>Project title</u> Hidden
▶ <u>Client</u> Hidden
▶ <u>Subject</u> Presentation of concept products designed by a group of nationally and internationally acclaimed designers and manufactured by Hidden
▶ <u>Year</u> 1999
▶ <u>Venue</u> International Furniture Fair and the Kölnische Kunstverein, Cologne, Germany

▶ <u>Duration</u> One week
▶ <u>Budget</u> EUR 113,000
▶ <u>Floor space</u> Fair: 100m²; gallery: 400m²
▶ <u>Estimated number of visitors</u> A few thousand
▶ <u>Most memorable aspect for the designers</u> We had total freedom to design the show as we saw fit; we didn't even need to show any drawings. We had never experienced this before. It was great.

Photography
Ewoud Traast

▶ <u>Page</u> 118
▶ <u>Project title</u> Hidden
▶ <u>Client</u> Hidden
▶ <u>Subject</u> Presentation of concept products designed by a group of nationally and internationally acclaimed designers and manufactured by Hidden
▶ <u>Year</u> 2000
▶ <u>Venue</u> Salone Internazionale del Mobile and Spazio Consolo, Milan, Italy
▶ <u>Duration</u> One week
▶ <u>Budget</u> EUR 68,000
▶ <u>Floor space</u> Fair: 45m²; gallery: 300m²
▶ <u>Estimated number of visitors</u> A few thousand
▶ <u>Most memorable aspect for the designers</u> During the gallery opening the Italians were so drunk and apparently so horny that they started jumping all over the king-size bra we had designed as part of the show.

132

Sources of quotations
Borges, Jorge Luis. 'There Are More Things,' *The Book of Sand* (Penguin Books, 1979).
Delauney, Robert. In *A Passion for Wings*, by Robert Wohl (Yale University Press, 1994).
Dent, J.M. In *The Penguin Book of Curious and Interesting Mathematics*, edited by David Wells (Penguin Books, 1997).
Hughes, Robert. 'The Threshold of Liberty,' *The Shock of the New* (Alfred A. Knopf, 1981).
Hugo, Victor. From Les Misérables. In *The Discoverers*, by Daniel J. Boorstin (Random House, 1983).
James, William. *A Dictionary of Philosophical Quotations,* edited by 'A.J. Ayer and Jan O'Grady (Blackwell Publishers, 1994).
Mallarmé, Stéphane. 'Le Livre, Instrument Spirituel,' translated by Michael Gibbs, *The Book, Spiritual Instrument*, edited by Jerome Rothernberg and David Guss (Granary Books, 1996).
Pascal, Blaise. *A Dictionary of Philosophical Quotations*, edited by A.J. Ayer and Jan O'Grady (Blackwell Publishers, 1994).
Pinker, Steven. *How the Mind Works* (Penguin Books, 1997).
Van Toorn, Jan. *Design Beyond Design*, edited by Jan van Toorn (Jan van Eyck Akademie, 1998).
Venturi, Robert. 'Mal Mots: Aphorisms—Sweet and Sour—by an Anti-hero Architect,' *Iconography and Electronics: Upon a Generic Architecture* (The MIT Press, 1996).
Wesseling, Janneke. 'Centraal Museum is "opgeleukt,"' *NRC Handelsblad* (December 12, 1999).

Bibliography

Books
Beeke, Anthon, *Dutch Posters 1961–1990*. BIS Publishers, Amsterdam, 1991. 105, 185, 173
Dean, Corinna, *Graphic Interiors: Spaces Designed by Graphic Artists.* Rockport, Gloucester, 2000. 144-155

Magazines
Staal, Gert. 'De stijlkamers van het nieuwe Centraal Museum' in *Items*, March/April 2000, 48–50
Thiemann, Robert. 'The Power of the Cliché' in *Frame*, September/October 1999, 32–39
Van Zijl, Ida. 'Tentoonstellingsontwerp steeds meer gericht op emoties' in *De Architect*, September 1999, 89
Gould, Mike. 'Hopes and fears' in *Affiche*, July 1994, 213
Ramakers, Renny. 'Geen doemdenken maar vooruitgang' in *Industrieel Ontwerpen*, April/May 1992, 10
De Michelis, Marco. 'Design and the environmental challenge' in *Arbitare*, April 1992
Rams, Dieter. 'Beyond the logic of consumerism' in *Ottogono*, March 1992, 29
McDonald, Edward. 'Designers with attitude' in *Print*, November/December 1991, 78
Vroege, Bas. 'Fotokunstenaars uit Zuid-Holland' in *Perspectief*, April/May/June 1986, 25–26

About the Author
Meghan Ferrill has an enduring interest in literature, especially
poetry, as well as in contemporary art and design. Born and raised
in Chicago, she has lived in Amsterdam since the mid-1980s,
where she works as a freelance creative writer. She has completed
numerous projects working either in collaboration with or for
graphic and industrial designers, architects, and builders. Her work
ranges from corporate communications, including websites and
vision statements, to essays, articles, and books on architecture
and design. In the period 1995–1998, she initiated and curated
a series of eight poetry and typography exhibitions in Amsterdam's
Stedelijk Museum.

Acknowledgments
Wim Beeren and Tracy Metz co-authored, *Marijke van der Wijst*,
edited by Martin Visser and Ineke Van Ginneke (010 Publishers,
Rotterdam, 1997).

Johannes Musset is thought to have designed the Droste cocoa tin
(circa 1900).

René Magritte painted *The Treason of Images*. The rights to the
reproduction in this book belong to Beeldrecht, Hoofddorp, the
Netherlands (2001).

Jacques Koeweiden and Paul Postma designed the advertisement
for Drum rolling tobacco (1995).

A CIP catalogue record for this book is available from the Library of Congress, Washington D.C., USA

Deutsche Bibliothek Cataloging-in-Publication Data
Traast + Gruson / [Frame magazine]. – Basel ; Boston ; Berlin : Birkhäuser; Amsterdam : BIS-Publ., 2001
(Frame monographs of contemporary architects)
ISBN 3-7643-6560-9
ISBN 90-806445-4-4

Printed in the Netherlands
987654321

136

TRAAST + GRUSON
Exposed
Frame Monographs of Contemporary Interior Architects

Publishers
Frame magazine
www.framemag.com
Birkhäuser – Publishers for Architecture
www.birkhauser.ch

Design
Peter Bil'ak

Author
Meghan Ferrill

Copy editor
Donna de Vries-Hermansader

Production
Tessa Blokland/*Frame* magazine

Color reproduction
Graphic Link

Photography of dividing pages
Ed Brandon

Printing
Hoonte Bosch & Keuning

Distribution Benelux, China, Japan, Korea and Taiwan
ISBN 90-806445-4-4
BIS Publishers
P.O. Box 15751
NL-1001 NG Amsterdam
The Netherlands
www.bispublishers.nl

All other countries
ISBN 3-7643-6560-9
Birkhäuser – Publishers for Architecture
P.O. Box 133
CH-4010 Basel
Switzerland
Member of the BertelsmannSpringer Publishing Group
www.birkhauser.ch